HARD WORK

CAN

KEEP YOU

POOR

WORK LESS AND ACHIEVE MORE BY FOLLOWING STRATEGIES THAT WORK

HARIB SHAQSY

COPYRIGHT NOTICE

Published year 2019, First Printing: 2020
ISBN 978-0-359-15728-0
www.haribshaqsy.com

The old saying goes:
"Love what you do, and you will never work a day in your life."

Foreword

This book reflects my own personal experience and opinion. None of the ideas and insights I have shared with you are perfect. This book documents my own results and the results that I have seen in the lives of many people.
However, I believe that if you follow and use the strategies and philosophies you learn in this book, you will be transformed.
This book contains proven steps and strategies on how you can increase your efficiency, through working smart than hard. The book provides an insight on why working hard is not all it takes to achieve success. It will explain why you should not work hard but stay efficient by working smart whenever the opportunity presents itself.
Ever since we were children, we've been taught about the virtues of hard work. The more work you put into something, the better you get at it. Schools, in particular, staunchly believe in testing students tens of times in a matter of months through class tests and what not. While it may seem that that's the way to go (that simple practice alone is not sufficient), it's certainly not the surefire way to success. Grueling hard work alone isn't the answer to all our problems. In fact, if that were the case, we would have a world full to the brim with successful people. Of course, this book teaches you how you be successful not just through hard work, which may be required if you wish to be someone important, but also through smart work.
This book describes how to make life meaningful and happy, through right living and smart working. It also speaks in detail the ways by which we can beautify our endeavor for smart work. Doing hard work to earn livelihood is also an essential part of life, but does not guarantee richness. Any noble thought even on upliftment of

mankind can only be successful through smart work. Our great plans in the life remain incomplete without some hard work associated with it, but only if you are in the right path and doing the right thing, otherwise, richness is uncertain. Creativity is a natural property of a person made by the 'Supreme Creator'; but generally it is seen that human tendencies are to take an easy life route. So it is found that even some elite class people may have an average positive attitude towards life than those of successful people.

No one can ever tell me that hard work alone is enough to make it in this life and be successful and rich. I know the truth. Sometimes, it doesn't make a difference how hard you work. Sometimes, you just can't make it.

Well, my story is not a surprise. It is not unique and it is not new. In fact, it may be very similar to your own.

I have studied hard and earned Certificates from different universities across the globe, such as in the United Kingdom and at the American University at Washington, in the United States of America.

Like most people, I have been working for many years. I have worked hard my entire adult life.

We lived on paycheck to paycheck (Salary).

Even being in middle class proved to be very stressful, and nothing near the perpetuated fantasy of success and comfort.

Like many people, when I was younger, I thought I could make it in the world if I just worked harder and harder.

I wanted to be promoted every few years and I wanted raises and benefit to increase.

Whenever the paycheck (salary) increases, life demands and expenses also increase, the price of commodities, rentals and other increases.

It keeps on going up, therefore, it is very difficult to save any money let alone be able to invest in any business.

Apart from working full-time, I also started working part-time as a freelancer.

I did website design and mobile app development for a few organizations, plus, other computer related work for whatever company needed me.

I thought that since my full-time job wasn't making me rich and happy, working part-time, extra hours would definitely be the solution.

So, I put too much more of my time into working to earn more. But, that was very hard and very exhausting, I ended up with colds, headaches and muscle pains and stressed, plus I was always in a bad mood. I soon realized that even by working two jobs, money issues never ended.

I thought, I would have a better chance to save and start my own business, but it was not until recently, I discovered that working hard alone is not the answer.

I was wasting too much of my time by providing many services.

Once I got married, I started working even harder and when my wife delivered our first child, I was determined to make some changes in our life for a better future. I kept on reading many books about personal finance, home businesses, self-help and personal development. I also attended seminars and workshops on these topics and became a student of determination.

I began to apply some of these ideas, and as of today, I am working towards that goal, I know it takes time, but it is worth the peace of mind.

I am much happier and life has changed dramatically from knowing and using these strategies that took me years to develop, discover and modify.

I don't work hard anymore and will never ever stress myself out again.

I spend some time researching, reading and writing my books, you can find some of my paperback books in stores and online.

Authoring is a very exciting business. This type of business brings passive income; an income that continues even if you stop writing more books.

Chapter 1

Hard Work

Forbes recently described a hard worker as: a self-starter and action-oriented person, who has a strong drive for success and has enough self-confidence to persevere when the going gets tough.

Well, that is per Forbes magazine.

But, why should you persevere and work hard at a place where the going gets tough?

When the going gets tough you find another job. Life is too short to live in pain. It is time to have a life and enjoy what you do.

Most people work hard because they believe that they have no other ways of getting an income. Therefore, they stay where they are.

Are you sure that you have no alternative?

What will hard work do for you if you are just another machine being paid less, working harder, and making others rich?

They know that hard workers always take full responsibility for all their work and actions, and realizing that there is no one else going to do their work better than a hard-working person.

So, they use them to get their work done and make themselves richer.

If you are a hard worker, why don't you find a better way to use that energy to your own advantage, such as running your own business?

I know that many of us stop trying because the first thing that comes into our mind is that we need money to start a business and how could we get financed?

This is where many people are stuck and never do anything about it If you are serious about starting a business, then you will find that financing.

It takes time and research, you need to visit many financial institutions and banks, ask and keep on knocking on doors until you make it.

Here are some ways to secure a loan:
Microloans: Try microloans from nonprofits or from the Small Business Administration (SBA). Since this is a microloan, funding may not be sufficient for all borrowers, but it is worth a try.

Personal Loans: Many new small-business owners secured financing through personal loans. There are a few things you need to know before you go for this option. You need to ask about the interest rates, some banks have very high interest for personal loans. So, do your own research.

Friends and Family: You can try borrowing money from friends or family. Many small businesses used this type of loan. It is not that easy, you need to really convince them to borrow money to you and tell them how you will be paying them back.
But it is always worth a try.

Credit Cards: Many small businesses used credit cards for funding their business startups, but it is important for you to know that credit cards are a very expensive way of financing a business, so do your research.

Crowd Funding: This type of funding has now become very popular. It is another way for small businesses to raise money. If you have a product and want to test the market, then this is the best place to start.
There are great sites like Kickstarter, which is the world's largest funding platform for creative projects and Indiegogo, which lets you request funds through online campaigns.

Grants: You can get startup funds for small business as grants from government agencies and private foundations. Try to do some research in your area.
Depending on where you live, because, each country has different funding organizations.

Investors or Partners: Search for an investor; someone that can invest in your business and take a share profit when the business is successful. You need to do your research before embarking on this type of investment. It has its own advantages and disadvantages.

Home Equity Loans: This is another type of loan, it is a loan against a house as collateral and is often considered a second loan and is based upon the equity in the property.
The lender will give you the money in full and it will have a fixed interest rate and repayment period.
This process takes time and can be risky if not maintaining the repayment. Plus, in western countries, you have to have a good credit score, in other countries, you are checked if your record is clean with banks.
There are many ways to get business loans. You have to do the research yourself.

In the USA, some people are cashing out their 401(k) and reverse mortgage etc.

Everyone has some form of talent and passion. Build upon your talents and passions. Many of us have more than one talent and many passions. With being passionate about what you do, you enjoy the work and you feel good doing it.
At least you know that the more effort you put into the business you love, the more income you put in your account. Plus, you enjoy doing what you love.

Making the Right Choice

You are probably working too hard because of the choices you made.

I love using the example below:

If you were given a choice to select a market to sell in, like either to open a gold retail shop or a produce market, what would you select?

Let's say you don't have to worry about financing.
I don't know about you, but I would choose selling gold over selling vegetables.

Why, you might ask?
I have nothing against vegetables or fruits, I love eating them, but selling them takes a lot of work.

Plus, they require proper storage and only have a few days before most of them spoil if not sold on time.
It takes more work, time, space and energy selling them than selling gold.

You definitely need to sell more mangos to make the same amount of profit as you would from an ounce of gold.
It takes a larger inventory, more space, more man or womanpower, and greater details to earn as much as selling gold.

On the other hand, gold, depending on the market price, can be sold by the grams/kg to have a greater earning potential with less, space, effort, time and you might pay less for the rent of space to do business.

Vegetables have health value, but when the same amount and weight of gold is put on a scale, the gold has a higher monetary value than the vegetables.

Unless, in a rare situation where there is a shortage of food, or the demand for a certain vegetable or fruit is extremely high then the price, and the value, will go up, but that is a very rare case.

Shift, Change and Grow

By now you are probably wondering why I am explaining my techniques with vegetables and gold.
Let me explain why.

The reason you chose this book is that, you wanted to know why hard work is not the key to wealth, why hard work alone will never make you rich.

Because, hard work is only a part of the process, and when applied in the wrong job that takes all your valuable time and work but does not pay much, then chances are, you will never be rich.

Look at your own situation; see were you fit in the example above.
We need to evaluate our current job or business.
We need to see if hard work and the time we are putting in our job are worth the effort. Is it really paying you well? Are you happy were you are?

If you are being paid less than you deserve and you put in a lot of effort, and work too hard, then it is time to wake up!
What determines your income is what job, service or business you're in and not how long and how hard you work. It is *"What you do, Where you do it, How you do it and with whom you do it"* that counts.

Who are you, a CEO of a company or a toilet cleaner? It's time to make a choice. You may need to wake up!
If you just work hard blindly, without taking some time to think and analyze your outcome and having no knowledge of the type of value it brings, and the type of person you become, then you will end up poor.

You can change if you make the decision to change, you are not a tree.

This is the reason why many people work very hard, because, they don't seem to have the will to change. They keep on doing what takes too much of their time, and working on the job they hate, while complaining that they don't have enough time to spend with their family and not enough money to pay their bills, and they haven't been on a vacation for years, plus they complain about everything, such as, the economy, the cost of living, the weather, the government and so on.

What they are working on requires more of their time and energy to get the result they are targeting for. Your financial situation will never change if you do not change. You need to make or do things differently so that you get the results you are looking for.

Taking Risks

To achieve any goal or become successful in anything, you must take some risks. You cannot achieve anything without taking risks.

Instead of worrying about losing your job or failing a business, do your due diligence, research and plan well, then take calculated risks.

If you do it with excitement and a positive attitude, then the risk will feel small.

Not all businesses are successful, so if yours is not, then try something else.

Find Your Passion

Well, I read many great stories of self-made millionaires and billionaires such as Mark Zuckerberg, Bill Gates and Warren Buffett and many others.

I believe they have one common thing that supported their journey towards wealth.

They have passion in what they do.
By being passionate in what you do, the work becomes pleasurable and fun to do.

When work is fun to do, then you are working less, because, it feels like you are having fun instead of working.

At the beginning of their journey, they did put some effort and energy into the business, because they know that after a while all will be fine and they delegate most of their work. Before they started any of their businesses, they did proper research and took some calculated risks.

With a proper business and marketing plan, they have seen the results before even starting the business. The viability of

the business is projected in the planning. That gives the courage to take the risk.
Because, successful people have passion for what they are doing, they enjoy doing it. They become wealthier.
Their efforts have paid off, and now they work fewer hours whenever they wish to.

Hard work is not a smart way to become rich, especially if done in the wrong job or business!
It's what you do and what value you bring with you.

Being passionate with what you do, can keep you richer than spending too many hours on a lower-paying job or even a job that you don't like, can keep you poor. It is your choice!
It is known that the longer you work without giving yourself a break the more unproductive you will become.
Giving yourself time to recharge and live your dreams will help you to do it the next day in a refreshed mind and body.
The more hours you spend the more damage you are doing to your health, and if you are unhealthy, you won't be able to put the energy and time into your work and the result will be a negative. You will be unhealthy and poor.

I like this quote from an unknown person posted in a forum.
"Smart work is done by using our mind and hard work is done by using our physical body."
Isn't that a good quote?

Review Your Strategy

You need to evaluate your current strategy.
I have seen people working as road or street cleaners, they
work very hard, they put in too many hours working.
They are the first people to be at work, they wake up earlier
than most of us and they are the last people to go home,
usually very late in the night.

They work in hot summers and cold winters, for many hours
a day, and they get paid less than most blue-collar workers.
Most of us work fewer hours compared to them and we get
paid much more.

Is it unfair?
Well, they are paid less, due to the type of job they are doing
and not the time, hard work and effort they are putting into
the job.
They are being paid for the value they bring with their work.
How valuable is that work compared to yours?
If hard work makes people rich, there would be many more
rich people.

Many people work very hard and deserve to be rich and that
would include me as well.
Unfortunately, hard work does not make you rich; *"What
you do, Where you do it, How you do it and with Whom
you do it"* that counts; the type of value you bring into the
marketplace and the type of person you become, that could
make you rich.

Such as *" Value, location, action and people."*

Increase Your Value

Here is a story of two college graduates, John and Sam.
These two young men graduated from the same university
with almost the same credits, the same grades. After their
graduation, they applied for jobs and both were hired at the
same company.

Sam worked very hard and sometimes takes work home.
Because of his hard work, he expects to get promoted to a
higher position and earn more money. He believes that he
deserves it more than many others in the same company,
including his friend John. On the other hand, John was the
guy that works within working hours, does not work too hard
and never take work home. He also like to read many
books, attends many types of presentations, seminars and
workshops. He keeps learning new things.

After about four years passed, John got promoted and Sam
was not. Sam got disappointed and felt that he was not given
a fair chance.

When Sam went to his supervisor to ask why he was not
promoted as his colleague John.

The supervisor, first, appreciated Sam's hard work. He said
to him that he knows that Sam is working harder than many,
including John. But the issue is that, the company decided to
stop all promotions until they sorted out the company's
losses, as profits had declined.

Sam asked, why then you promoted John? The supervisor,
replied, that they needed to keep John from leaving the
company, because, he came up with a new strategy again that
we believe will solve this issue.

"What exactly?" Sam asked.

The supervisor explained to Sam that, a couple of years ago, if it was not for John, then this company would have been closed and we would have not been here now.

As we are now in need of his assistance to overcome this issue again, we do not want him to leave now.

"John is the one that came up with an idea and a strategy that saved our company.

John did a lot of research and came up with a great plan that we have been using. We are moving forward and the result was very good until now while things are changing, we need to change as well.

We have to promote John to keep him from leaving the company. So, would you like us to remove John and put you in his position?"

Sam could not answer that question.

When you are working for any company or organization, if you always do what you are asked to do and nothing else, then you are not playing it as a leader and getting promoted is very slim plus you are replaceable.

However, if you become more valuable to the company and help the company increase their profits with your ideas and reduce their expenses and make work easier, then you will be irreplaceable and probably get paid more to keep you from quitting.

Imagine that, you gave your company a strategy that transformed the company's operation and increases its profit from $10 million a year to $50 million a year. Can the company raise your salary ten times or twenty times more?

Let's say, you were receiving $2000 per month, could you get an increase to $20,000 or $40,000 per month? The answer is yes! They will pay as much to keep you from leaving the company.

If you increase your value, you will attract better income and you could become richer and work less.

To increase your value, you need to read as many books as you can, to research more and to attend lectures, trainings and whatever information that relates to your company's process and your job.

You need to increase your knowledge on a continual basis. If you stop learning, you stop growing.

The Need to Change

A large percentage of people are currently employed and keep their jobs to support themselves and their beloved families. Most jobs that people are employed in require a lot of hard work and putting more hours than most people want to work into them.

Jobs that most do, does take a lot of their valuable time, the time that could have been used to spend with their loved ones and to relax and unwind.

If your current job is taking away your time for living the life that you've always wanted, then It is time to find another way of obtaining an income without spending too much time doing it.

If you take some time to search and look around, you can find another way of earning an income.

What you need is, first to recognize that you need to change, then you need to put some action to search and research for better opportunities or best of all is to start your own business, everything else will follow.

Chapter 2

How important is Money?

Some people say that money is not everything, but I see money as an important thing in our life and for survival in this world.

Unless you are lost on an island and there is no way to get back, and not much clean water, plus no food and you have with you, billions of dollars. That money will be useless to you.

You would rather trade all your money for food, water and getting your life back.
So, money is important only when you can use it.
Some people believe that money is the root of all evil, and that belief will keep them poor.
If money is the root of all evil, then why do so many religions accept donation, charity and volunteer, what are they working for?
Are they working for free?
If money is bad, then why are you working?
I believe that, money is an idea, which is backed by confidence.

Rich and wealthy know how to play the game of money.
Those are entrepreneurs who are willing to give some of their money to buy other people's time.
They use people as so called "employees" to work for them and make them richer.

If we keep on trading our time for money, then we are enslaved by it.

We are working so hard making our bosses rich, and we keep on doing it without any thought about it.

You cannot be wealthy if you swap your precious time for just money.

Most of us were told when we were young that, if we put a lot of effort into school or college, study hard, get good grades in school then we can easily get a good job.
Not many of us got that job easily, plus many of us did not get the job that we planned for, so we ended up working at a job that we hate, to just barely survive.
Plus, we were told that, if we work very hard, then, we will make a lot of money and the chances are we will become richer.

Well, I have yet to see someone who did that and became rich.
Using time for money has great limitations, plus how much time can you be working in a day while working for someone else?

Time cannot be bought and cannot be created, so we are limited to the twenty-four hours in a day, while half of it is for rest and sleep.

Even Lawyers and Doctors suffer from this limitation; they earn high salaries, but very few of them could reach a wealthy status in their lifetime.

Most of them are swapping time for money.
When they stop working for some reason, such as due to sickness or other circumstances, they stop making money.

A physician as well, is paid only by the number of patients he can see at a time and limited to how many hours he can work in a day.

This includes dentists and lawyers, unless, they employ some staff to do part of their work, then it would be more profitable, but there are expenses that come with having employees that a small business cannot afford.
So, the only way they can get richer is, by running their business and letting others work for them.

That way, they will have more time for themselves.
With this strategy, they can open as many branches of their business as they desire, if they have enough money to do so.

Passive Income Model

Having too much money does not mean that you are rich.
Being rich is all about how you think about making money, and how financially literate you are.
Look at an example of Warren Buffet or Bill Gates. If you take away everything they own and let them start from nothing, they will eventually become rich again within two to three years.

This is because, they are financially intelligent and they have great knowledge of how to make a lot of money. This is due to their mind set as well.
On the other hand, I have heard about some people winning millions in a lottery and then become poor in just a about five or six years.

This is due to their poor mentality and poor financial intelligence.
If you understand how to build wealth, then you are already wealthy.

If a person earns $200,000 a year and spends $200,000 a year, then he is not rich. If another person earns about $50,000 a year, he spends $30,000, saves $5,000 and invests $15,000 that makes him a passive income, then he is rich.

Rich people save and invest on a passive income that pays them even if they stop working.
If you want to work less and increase your income, you need to have a passive income model.
With this model, you get paid even if you are not working any more.

For example: an author of a book.
Authors who write once and get paid for as many copies of their work printed and sold repeatedly without any more work from them.
Many authors I know have made millions of dollars with this type of model.

Another example is a realtor.
They rent apartments and get paid repeatedly while the tenants are renting them.
Many realtors I know that have made millions of dollars and some have made billions using this type of model, people like Robert Kiyosaki, a known entrepreneur and a real estate expert, plus many others such as artists and musicians.
They get paid for copies of their work. Musicians record their work and can sell as many copies of their work without doing it again.
Do it once and get paid more than once.
Many musicians became very rich using this model.
Your ability to earn is unlimited if you free yourself from wasting your valuable time working too hard to earn money.
If you look around you will find a lot of businesses that use this type of model and strategy.

Find one that will earn you a recurring income, such as leasing an office space or building etc.

Become an Investor.

Mutual funds, bonds and stocks are some of the investments that require less work from you and the earning ability is unlimited, depending on the success of the investment.
This is another way of making money while you are asleep.
But, being an investor needs good knowledge of the subject due to its unpredictability. You need to be very knowledgeable of the subject before you put your money into this type of business.
You can enroll yourself in a course online that will teach you about investing. There are hundreds of courses about many different businesses, many for free. Just make your decision to learn as much as you can before you embark on this business.

Every business is learnable. If you are serious about starting one, you can find the required training courses online and offline. You must do your research.

Build Websites that Sell

Another way of passive income is through an online website to sell either your own product or as an affiliate and earn money while you are either on vacation, walking on the beach, or sleeping.
You could use a freelancer or outsource the work and have your business running in a few weeks.
It is another way to work less.
Building a website that sells affiliate products is not difficult. You can use freelancers that are available online to build it for you.

Even if in the start, it makes you $10/day, remember that's over $300/month to start with and if advertised well, then the earnings will be more.

If that website is replicated to 5 more of the same or different products, then your earnings can be almost five times, depending on how valuable your business is. You could earn i.e. $300 x 5 = $1500/month or even more. But, this depends on the type of business, if it is replicable or not. Some business can be replicated and some not. Do not limit your income because of time.

Get started now and enjoy life without working too hard, start building an income stream that does not depend on your precious time or your presence.
Your life will never be the same; you will get paid while you are on a vacation or spending time with your family etc.
Do not get me wrong here; I am not suggesting that you leave your current job before having an alternative income.
At the beginning, you need to get a good job that will pay you enough and save for a business startup.

If that takes too long, then, try to get a business loan, many banks and financing companies will give business loans, you need to search in your area.

Most of us need to work for someone else to earn enough to invest for a business startup.

Once the business runs well and can pay for itself then you can decide to put more of your effort and time into it and then leaving your current job would be a wise decision.

Work on Yourself

If you really want to make more money or even become richer, then you must work on yourself first.
Working on yourself, by improving your knowledge on subjects that pertain to your business, how to be an effective salesman, effective marketer and all that is required for you to achieve that goal and run a business successfully.

Most of us hate this hectic lifestyle, we get up very early in the morning and get stuck in traffic, get to work and make someone else rich, spend less time with our family and at the end of the month, have less and less money to save and enjoy.

Our needs these days are growing bigger than ever and the price of commodities are going up and up, while our salaries have remained the same for many years and if by some chance our salary is increased, the price of commodities and other utilities are already high by that time.

We are blindly going through all this without even trying to analyze and change, because, we believed that we have no other choices, we believe that we have no alternative and we must provide food for our children and pay our bills.
Many of us got stuck in this same loop for years.
I realized that later in life.

This is not what we are here for. We deserve better in life than that.
I began researching and reading so many books, attended many seminars and took online courses and more.
I worked on myself first.

I then got my own online business running, while tweaking and changing, and it keeps on getting better and better.

I was also a webmaster, and I did freelance web design and mobile app development for many organization, but now I am putting my energy into my online businesses.
They are part of my passion.

I don't feel like I am working but having fun instead. It is like playing for me, I do it for fun and get paid for it.
This is one of examples of working less and earning more.
If you have any experience on website design, graphic design, scripting and programming or even mobile app design, then you have real treasure in you.

You can start working in your spare time at home using the internet, and earn a lot of money doing what you love or what you have a passion to do.

You can use websites like Elance.com which is now called Upwork.com and fiverr.com and many other freelancer websites to join as a web developer, programmer, book editor, writer, graphic designer, SEO, Music creator and many other categories that you can select.

You can bid whatever amount that you feel that the project you chose to do will cost, depending on the work and time you put on it.

I have earned enough extra income running my own home business using online services as mentioned above. All you need is a few hours a day.

There are many other online businesses you can do, just visit websites like fiverr.com and a few others plus search Google and you will find many and see what other sellers are doing on that website, and see if you find anything that you have experience doing and start your own.

It is your own awareness that is required of you to know whether you need to make the necessary change or not. You must know the problem before you can ever try to change it.

If you want to have a better financial lifestyle, you need to leave that job that takes all your valuable time; you need to start living now.
I can't recommend any better book on running a business than that of Mr. Robert Kiyosaki titled "Cash Flow-Quadrant," you need to read it.
It will change the way you think about making money.
I read it a few times and I have learned so much from that book.

Bad thing about being an employee is that you are trading your valuable time for money, it is short-term, and has limited income and will not pay you much after you leave that job.

Even when you get paid a little more, your commitments, expenditure, and even your taxes increase.
There are many rich and creative people like entrepreneurs, such as investors, and business owners who are living a life of freedom, also they pay less tax compared to a person working on a job.

As the saying goes about the word JOB... "Just Over Broke"
If you wish to be rich and work less, you need to be an entrepreneur, you need to invest in a business; you need to start your own business.

Be Creative, You Need Good Ideas

As an entrepreneur, you need to have good ideas.
If you find something that has great value, and has a lot of demands, then the chances are it will sell well.

To be successful as an entrepreneur, you must stop working for money. You must have the money working for you.
Work to get the experience required first to run your own business and use that money to pay for the startup of your business or secure a loan, a business loan.

After all, goes well, then you must stop trading your time for the money and start managing your business instead.
Find a company that will teach you all the ins and outs of that business or trade. Get to learn as much as you can about how and what they are doing with the type of business you want to run.

Not everyone will succeed as a good entrepreneur; it is not that easy, but you can do it only if you are willing to put some effort in the beginning and keep on tweaking and adjusting it until you make it.
Most people give up too soon; you need to be persistent to be successful.

It also requires financial capabilities and creative mindset, and proper people to work with you and get the job done.

Every Problem has a Solution

If we look around us, we observe what problems need a solution or need to be overcome, we then have an opportunity to find the solution to that problem and people will be willing to pay for the solution we provide for them.

This is one type of business that made many people millionaires and billionaires, people like Mark Zuckerberg, Bill Gates, and Warren Buffett plus many other millionaires and billionaires.

They saw a need and they provided a solution.

Opportunity Recognition

You should be open-minded and learn about any opportunity that shows up.

If you are not open-minded, then you could miss such opportunities and other great possibilities from it.

If you miss the opportunity and someone else does get it, you will be unhappy and will give up trying.

You have better chances to gain on an opportunity if you take some risks, and then make the best out of the opportunity even if the result is below your expectations.

Organize and Work Less

If you are still employed, there are many tricks that can be applied to achieve more productivity with no stress or irritation.

One of the tricks is preparing a list of all expected tasks, then removing all tasks that do not require your intervention or are not urgent. This trick allows you to concentrate on the important tasks and relieves you from possible distractions. When you set daily goals, and focus on the main goal, it contributes in keeping track of things without losing focus. In addition, it removes the possibility to waste time on processes or tasks that will not favor the goal.

You need to find your productivity peak periods; it is one important component to find out. It is not possible to have energy all the time. Therefore, it is important to make the most of production time in the time when you are more energetic.

A good work environment is important and should be considered properly, because, it has direct effect on the resulting outcomes.

Your focus can be taken away by so many distractions if you did not prepare work schedules; therefore, it will add time. This could further lead to temporary deviation from the total work schedules that were made to achieve the goal.

Chapter 3

Change Your Thinking

If a positive thinking attitude is in place, we will only have a
few hindrances or obstacles that could serve as problems,
and in fact, we will view them from a more positive angle.
We must have a can-do mentality, it also takes perseverance
and practice, but worth it.

The following are some helpful tools to encourage a positive
mentality and reduce work stress:
In both explored endeavor and capability, we must have
strong faith, always. Perhaps, this is the most vital element to
have a successful business experience. Faith will be the guide
that we need to overcome challenges and impossibilities.
We should be knowledgeable to a greater extent. This
positively contributes to the goal getting mindset. It will be
easy to handle different tasks when there is acceptable
knowledge, and there will be nothing like a daunted
experience but there will be advantages to enjoy.
We need to be go-getters, be bold and never shy. Shyness
dampens every attempt to be open to any opportunity.
Therefore, there is a need to keep the go-getting trait under
control.

When we want success, looking the part is recommended.
This is not dressing expensively or use of expensive
accessories but rather showing confidence needed to be sure
that other people are encouraged well enough to relax and
convinced by our point of view during discussion.
We must know how to impress people with our knowledge
and personality without being proud or rude. If this is

observed, there won't be solicitation of anything from anybody.

Achieving Wealth

Here are some of the strategies that are known in obtaining a good income.

If you are self-employed or working as an employee, you can decide to improve your skills, by taking more trainings and reading more on the subject to improve and become more efficient instead of working hard. Then you end up working less and earning more.

If you are an artist, programmer, designer, inventor or other professional, you can use your creative mindset to explore new avenues of income.
If you are a manager, business owner, executive, a leader, you can use people and other resources at your disposal to generate new streams of income.

You can use your spare time to write an e-book regarding your experience, expertise, and the critical aspects of your profession. If you can help people in resolving issues related to your field of expertise, you would also get return favor in terms of steadily increasing sales of your e-book.
Computer programmers or other professionals with a creative mindset can use their talent to design, develop and launch their own products and services rather than working for their employer.

People with a business mindset can explore the possibility of earning more revenues from their existing or potential investment in real estate. For example, you can pool resources to buy houses with good profit potential or work on cheap houses to improve their resale value and close deals with good return. It may require very little efforts in terms of research or resource mobilization to explore and execute profitable ideas.

If you are unable to arrange financing, explore the viability of financing your projects through bank loans. You can take a grant, pool resources or collaborate with other investors to finance a profitable venture.

You can choose any method or strategies to make more money. If you are determined to change your destiny, you will face no shortage of opportunities to realize your financial goals.

You must keep on searching and asking.
We will discuss more on the power of "Asking" in the next section.

The Power of Asking

Most successful people ask. Asking is a very powerful way to learn about anything.

If you do not ask because, you are either afraid or feel too shy to ask, then you must try to change that feeling, because, it does not serve you well.

If you ever wanted help, such as to have money to start your business or solve your current problems and fulfill your needs, you need to start asking.

People do not know what you need until you ask.
Most people are afraid to ask due to many things. They may be afraid of rejection, being laughed at or made to look cheap and inferior.

You can ask for whatever you want, sometimes you get and sometimes not, but if you never tried asking, the chances are you won't get what you wanted.

Here are many ways to ask for what you want.
You should be very clear to what you really want.
Ask the right person who has what you need.
Ask the right question without mixing it with another requirement, just for that one thing.

Ask with positive attitude, to let the other person get to feel that your question is genuine. Remember, people can read your feelings through your posture, your voice and attitude. Persistence is the key to a successful asking, if one person says no, maybe he/she was in a bad mood, then keep on trying with the same person again later in a better mood, or try another person and so on, until you are successful.

Take Action Now

Whatever your dreams, plans and desire, they will never be achieved if you do not take action.
When you start doing by taking action, you will generate more ideas about that action that will keep you moving forward to achieve your goal.

You will automatically be aligned with the things and people with similar goals.
As the saying goes, "A thousand miles' journey starts with a single step."

Whatever knowledge you have will not get you paid unless you take some action and do something about it.
You get paid for the service you provide, for the product you sell and for the ideas you formulate, it must have some action to be recognized.

44

Many people avoid taking action because of fears, they never get what they really wanted because, and it is that uncomfortable feeling that they are running from.

Many fears are due to something unknown, it is when you have not much knowledge of something that you want to achieve. The best way to fight this fear is to build some confidence by learning more about something that you wanted to achieve. Research and learn more about the subject.

When you have enough information about it, then you gain some confidence, and then just do it and the fear will begin to fade.

Seeking Advice

Whenever you want to seek advice, seek it from the right person.

When you seek advice about your health, ask your doctor. If you are seeking advice about money, find someone who is doing better than you financially and ask for advice. If you are seeking advice for your car, ask the car mechanics. Many people seek advice about money from their parents, it is OK if the parents are already doing very well with their finance, but if they are not, then it would be better if they ask a financial adviser or someone that is doing much better that them and follow their advice.

Your parents or friends might give you advice because, they wanted to help you, but if they are not doing what they are advising you, then you should not take their advice.

Attracting Wealth

Pretend that you have already achieved what you wanted to achieve, such as becoming rich, having that house you've been longing for or having the vacation you dreamed of. Our subconscious mind cannot tell the difference between real and imaginary events. Therefore, take this opportunity to visualize whatever you love to achieve and see what will happen.

There are many studies done about our subconscious and how our thoughts are shaping our world.

The Power of Failure

Failure is a temporary defeat, it is there to teach you something and make you stronger.
It is often a blessing in disguise.
It usually gives us courage to reach our goals.

Many successes come with some crisis, the more the crisis the greater the opportunity of advancement.
Remember, when you fail, you are becoming wiser and stronger. Learn from your failures.

Chapter 4

What is Smart work exactly and how different is it from hard work?

What goes through your mind when you hear the word 'smart'? I'm guessing something along the lines of intelligent or clever. Well, working smart is exactly that. You work not with sheer brute force but by being intelligent about every action. In other words, instead of slogging through some tedious job, you look for a way to make it easy for yourself.

Let's take data entry, for example, a job that is mostly reserved for interns in companies. It's as boring as it sounds. In it, your job is to enter data, most often off of hardcopies of forms that have been filled by people who are almost always in a hurry, into some database. As a result, they barely write legibly, plus a guessing data entry with mistakes. Therefore, data entry is not for smart workers.

How to work smart and not hard

Smart working is an inborn quality of a person to do better than others within the same time period. Some competitive feeling or intuition might force a person to do better than others. They do great work as they love to do and perform by their perseverance. One understands the job before telling to others and synergizes. Synergy is coordinating with all working groups on the project.

What is Being Rich in your Views?

We all have our own view of what being rich means. And with that view comes our own prejudices, beliefs, notions, feelings, thoughts and habits.

And, of course, it's the actions we take in life that determine the results we achieve.

You have choices in life every single day. To start a business or keep doing what you're doing. To study hard and search for the knowledge you need to succeed or gossip and play video games. To work out or watch TV. You always have choices. Are you making the right choices consistently enough to get where you want to go?

Being rich is only what you view it.

Richness could mean absolutely nothing to you or it could mean something.

But you could make it mean something by the way you think of it.

Maybe you make it mean people who are rich are bad. Maybe you make it mean being rich will make you happy. Maybe you make it mean being rich will make you shallow. Begin to notice the meaning you have attached to being rich, to money, and to finances in general.

Whatever you make it mean, let it go for now and see.

Just let go of your view of what being rich means. You see, there's no power if you say people who are rich are bad because then you will lose out on the possibilities of relationships with people who happen to be rich. And if your best friend gets rich, you will think he is a bad person because he happens to be rich. How messed up is that?

Beliefs have the power to transform our lives or trap us in a prison of our own self-imposed limitations.
But many people let little negative beliefs run their entire lives... and they never realize why they just can't seem to scrape by enough money to do what they really want to do with their lives. Don't let that be you!

If you're feeling stuck financially right now, chances are that the heart of your problem has nothing to do with money at all. It has everything to do with your beliefs.
Why limit yourself financially?
You've got to realize you will never have power over your financial life unless and until you give up the meanings you have put on objects, situations, and things outside of yourself. You must realize that you are in control of your life, in every way, in every situation, now, in the past, in the future and always.

You are all-powerful. You are a creators.

Chapter 5

Positive and Proactive Attitude towards Life

I know that our topic is about how not to work hard, but that does not mean never work hard, it means work hard only on jobs that can pay you more, the jobs that have more market value.

Therefore, hard work is required as well.

Progress in any sphere of life is depending on positive and proactive attitude of a person performing the work. Positive attitude develops creativity in a person, explores various means of doing a work and his performance meets success.

When one decides to achieve everything by shortcuts avoiding hard work there in, the result might be a failure.

One should earn more and thus be a giver not a liberty on others performing no duty and expecting high achievements is not right attitude.

Life is about giving and receiving, about enjoying your works and taking care of those who raised you, your family when they get old. Sometimes a lazy person instead of working hard, might expect a comfortable life by external source of gratitude such as blessings of Guru etc. She might give proof of the blessings; she had been receiving from any such source. But we can see for ourselves, there are atheist who do not believe in God or fate but still get things done perfectly through their determination and hard work.
An agnostic might argue to know the logic behind any such assumptions. Like assuming that God is there to feed us or

solve our problems. Sure God feeds us but only if we are willing to work for it.

God loves us all, but it is our duty to work for a living, he gave us everything we need to be able to take care of ourselves.

Anyone to live a life with luxury, without losing her integrity, will have to be a progressive thinker, good planner, with positive attitude and hardworking capabilities. Attitude is key to advance one's interest. If the attitude is not in right direction, there cannot be achievements.

Attitude of a person decides where to go. Secondly aptitude or capabilities are to require to accomplish a goal. One can choose higher goal if aptitude permitted. Aptitude can weigh the possibility and then putting one's capabilities to work is mandatory. A genuine desire; (Attitude) with practical approach and hard work can give the final success in perfect competition of goal. Working with right attitude on a job gives mental satisfaction and less chances of mental depression.

One who thinks possibility of starting a new venture with good planning, proactive working till end, can accomplish it successfully. Some people with reactive attitude may give up halfway and give various reasons for their failure like circumstances, poor resources etc. The achievements come other way round to those who work from dawn to dusk without caring that others are enjoying the time in entertaining themselves.

Is Hard Work Good or bad?

Not all hard work is bad, there is an exception to this.

When I say hard work can keep you poor, I meant that, you will remain poor when you work in a job that provides less value to the market place, a job that has no means of growth, a job that pays you enough to survive, a job that has no potential to promote you and to increase your earnings so that you can save and invest in your future, such as investing in your own business and a job that requires you to put extra hours without getting paid more.

But when your job brings a lot of value to the market place, and you get paid well, you should work much smarter and by all means if you prefer working harder, then that's fine.

Many countries around the world encourages working hard, they encourage their citizens to work harder, which led them to successful inventions in different fields.
Some great initiatives taken by governments helped people to grow through their right attitude and hard working. One such example is of China; the synergy between Chinese government initiatives and her citizen's hard work with determination improved county's economy in the past.

At one times lower rated by international standards becomes a top economy today. Today Chinese are in position of extending conditional help to the poor nations. How have they turned deserts onto Greenway resort, agricultural farming field, and beautiful fruit garden by their right attitude and hard work together; Today Chinese companies are also earning by recycling and reusing items to a maximum level.

They are proud of these achievements and enjoy the recognition of same throughout the world.

Some other countries' history read; like Germany and Japan, ruined completely their economy in wars, came back with thunder after their citizens planning and doing very hard work and are rated among top, developed nations of the world with the highest GDP.

A small country like Singapore, had a great water problem at one time but their government had a plan and people did hard work, developed water reservoir for preservation of Rainwater, are having surplus water today. They made mark progress in Tourism sector and developed their economy to world class.

On the contrary, history is there of number of exceptions where people adopted negative approach and became liberty on others. Whenever they found limited success, misused their achievements in wasteful idle living. Spending costly hours in drinking, gambling and all bad habits, made their life worst. They didn't develop their families as well but kept blaming the society or government for their misgivings and failures. They wanted things to come by luck or shortcuts without working which was not possible. Some even go to the extent of learning how to rob others' earned money and grab their possessed wealth. Through study of social sciences, we find that some such disillusioned and derogatory people had been forming dangerous groups and acted arrogantly against the interest of others in past and continuing even in today's world. These people might found things like religions for creating different opinions and means of confronting with each other.

There are people who only fight for their rights. The fact is that one must do the duties properly before asking for her rights. Laziness and living with honor does not go together.

Working Smarter has many advantages

Smart work is more focused on result orientation. It is applying your skills in right direction to reach your goals in shorter time. Smart working person will foresee the problems on the way and find remedial action. Only hard working may not help a person to accomplish his or her job successfully as there might be hurdles on the way. Both are complimentary to each other's' functions.

A big profit is possible in short time by making proper use of resources and generate new opportunities for unemployed youth. It will open the door for livelihood of many people working for the company.

Smart work aims at achieving goals with quality and more production within limited time. Doing smart work allows to have time for things like exercise, spending time with family etc.

Impossible act could be made possible by practical approach and smart working.
Huge log of unfinished work can be cleared in minimum time.

There is a vast difference between the living style of smart working person and a hard working persons, in due course that changes their wellbeing.

When a person earnings comes by successful smart work, it gives an immense pleasure and one hates to adopt foul means to be wealthy.

Beside all this; success on a project would bring good earnings and psychological gain and enhanced happiness. She develops confidence in earning herself and can never cheat others for petty gains. Such person might become patriarch or a leader.

Common Misconceptions Surrounding the Dichotomy between Hard Work and Smart Work

What goes through your mind when you think of a millionaire CEO of some successful company? What do you think his daily routine consists of? It wouldn't be surprising if you thought that they don't have much to do all day, that the momentum of their initial success sustains itself without them. The truth, however, is that they work exceptionally hard even when they've reached multi-millionaire status. The most successful CEOs work for 14 to 18 hours a day at times and they've even been reported to start their days at 5 in the morning (while most of us have a hard time waking up at 7).

You needn't look far for the proof. Take Elon Musk, for example. He's a billionaire entrepreneur who started off with next to nothing. He toiled for 2 years before even getting a glimpse at success. So dedicated was he that slept and bathed in his office as he had dedicated himself completely to his work. People like Elon Musk don't just work smart by making use of all available technologies and services, they outrun the competition by pushing themselves beyond the limit. Their strategy isn't based on brute force alone (far from it, in fact). They understand the fact that in order to stay ahead of the pack, they have to outmaneuver the other contenders through the combination of brains and sheer willpower.
Grow or Die!

Note: I hope you do not get confused with what the title of this book says, "Hard Work Can Keep You Poor" It is clearly explained the reason for that title in the first chapters.

We gave you exact reason as this.

It is *"What you do, Where you do it, How you do it and with whom you do it"* that counts. If you meet these statement above then working hard is fine.

The law of the Universe

There is one simple law in the universe that most people are either unaware of or ignore to their own detriment. That law is this: You are either growing or dying
Do you know how scientists find the age of a pine tree?
They count the rings of growth.

Each year, the tree grows and creates a fresh ring of newly grown wood every year without fail. Some years the rings are big and some years they are small due to environmental changes, but a living tree always grows a new ring each year. When a pine tree fails to grow a new ring one year, you know the tree is dead. That's it. There is no middle ground. There are no pine trees that live but decide not to grow. Their nature is to grow or die. Just like you. Your nature is to grow or die. Growth is proof that you're alive.

Likewise, human beings are meant to grow every year. We are meant to grow intellectually, spiritually, emotionally, and in every area of our life. You are either growing or dying. This law may be easiest to see in the world of business.

When you see a business that's growing, it's doing well and everything is great. But when you see a business that fails to grow, you know it is dying.

It's clear to the people inside the business that something is not right. The best employees tend to leave when a business starts dying, and the business usually goes bankrupt or is sold

56

off. Of course, we all know of an amazing business turnaround where a floundering business became a thriving, growing company once again. These turnarounds only happen because someone in the organization decided to grow the business again instead of worrying about maintaining the status quo.

In your life, if you feel like you're floundering, stuck, or just not achieving the success you want, realize that it will only turn around when you decide to start growing again.
I know you are ready to grow because you are reading this book! Let's keep growing together.

Awareness is Key

Despite what you may hear in the news about the economy or finances, today is the easiest time to get rich there has ever been in the history of the world!
Here are just a few of the reasons why:
Information is more readily available today through the internet to just about anyone, anywhere at anytime
The internet has created an opportunity for anyone to start an online business for less than $100—for those who are willing to learn how.

Today, find an opportunity to increase your income and increase your wealth. They're everywhere. All you have to do is look.

Even if you just start with a $5 transaction, so what? That could be the beginning of the next billion-dollar company! After all, McDonald's earns billions of dollars a year selling one $5 meal at a time. Every business starts with its first dollar earned. Start by earning your first dollar and then worry about growing. Your awareness will grow as you begin to take action.

That Dirty Little Word Called Discipline

What drives some people to begin and others to never even try? Discipline.
Discipline is the ability to get yourself to begin.
Discipline allows you to do something even though you're afraid.
Discipline is what separates the successful and the great from the unsuccessful and the ordinary.
Discipline is a habit.
Why Develop Discipline?

When you develop discipline in your life and finally begin doing all the things you know you should be doing, your life will change forever.

You will find yourself becoming happier, stronger and wiser. You will start living a life with more meaning and purpose. You will find that your actions affect others in your life and have ripples that continue on toward infinity and return back to you what you put out.

When you develop discipline, you begin playing big. You become a powerful, positive influence in the world.
Why is discipline so hard? Why is it hard to do what we know we should do? Why does it seem hard to succeed sometimes? Fear.

Start today. Focus on your discipline. Write down what you want to do, what you need to do to accomplish your goals, and begin today to get it done.

Self-Mastery

Discipline is a part of self-mastery. Self-mastery allows you to do the difficult but important things in life. It allows you to deal with any obstacle life puts in front of you.
Your greatest obstacle in life doesn't lie outside of you—it lies within you. What's holding you back from getting rich, has nothing to do with the economy or your education or anything outside of yourself. It's your own fear, self-doubts, negative thoughts, and bad habits and self-sabotage that keep you from living the life you want.

Focus on self-mastery. Become an "enlightened warrior." An enlightened warrior is one who conquers oneself.
When you've mastered yourself, there is nothing else to worry about. Everything else is becomes simple.

If the economy gets worse, if you lose your job, if some other financial setback occurs, it won't stop you from success if you have self-mastery. You'll be able to focus on what's important. You'll understand how to begin to pick up the pieces and get moving in the direction of your dreams. Without self-mastery, you'll think the setback means you're not meant to be rich. You'll focus on your worries, struggles and fears instead of focusing on what to do to improve your life.

What's Easy to do is Easy Not to Do

It's easy to wake up early and exercise. It's easy to plan your day by writing down the 6 most important things to do. It's easy to save at least 10% of your money and invest it wisely. It's easy to be rich.

The problem is that it's also easy not to do the activities that will get you where you want to go. Your challenge then is to start doing the important activities starting today.

Today is the only day that matters. Get rid of your tomorrows and some days and start today. If you found one good idea in this book, put it to use today. Set your goals. Write down your plan for tomorrow. Get that book. Go to that seminar. Do it today!

It's funny how people say, "they're just rich because they're lucky. Look how easy it is for them."

The truth is, it's easy for all of us. Last time you tried, it was pretty easy to buy a book and read it. It was pretty easy to sign up for a seminar and attend it. It was easy to get up early and go running. It was easy to write down your plan for the day and make the calls you had to make Making progress and moving in the right direction isn't rocket science.

It's easy!

But don't let that fool you; it still takes discipline. Every day. Discipline is not a one-time thing. It's an ongoing process of doing what you know you should do and doing your best. How do you do that? You must consciously choose to do the most productive thing you can.

Plan it out, write it down, and get to work. If you really accept this way of life, you will no longer find any need to watch TV, waste time or to feel sorry for yourself. You'll be too busy having fun being a successful, happy and rich person.

We must learn to manage our time by focusing on priorities. At any point in time, you may have a dozen possible things you could do, but only one thing you could do that is the most important. And that's what you should do.

Have a Dream, then Team Up and Collect

Everything starts with a dream. An idea. Once you have that idea that dream, that burning desire to do something, whether it be to start your own business, become a millionaire, or become a sensational public speaker, everything changes.

No matter what your dream is, you need a team of skilled, enthusiastic, and helpful people to assist you in making it happen. There is no such thing as a self-made millionaire. Humans are infinitely more powerful together than alone, assuming the right people are on the team.

The Best Things in Life Must Be Discovered

If you truly want to get something amazing out of life, you have to discover it for yourself.

If you just buy all the junk they advertise on TV, you'll have a mediocre life at best. If you buy only the food advertised on TV, you will be unhealthy, sick and die early. If you buy only the investments advertised by the major banks, you will face financial disaster when the next market crash comes if not before.

You Must Be Moved

When you hear about others who are suffering, how do you react? Do you see people struggling in life? Could you help them in some way? According to T. Harv Eker, Entrepreneurship is solving problems for people at a profit. What problems do you see that you could help solve? When you are moved enough to drive you into action, that is when you will truly begin striving for riches and greatness. When you are moved enough to solve someone else's problem and forget about your own, then you will begin your journey to greatness. That's all entrepreneurship is. Solving problems for others.

Most rich people don't get up early and stay up late just to make an extra dollar. They get up early and stay up late because they are so touched that they are driven to serve others as best they can.

Chapter 6

Ways to work smart

In fact, success takes more than just a combination of hard and smart work. It requires the taking of risk, ingenuity, vision and a touch of luck. However, there are techniques that you can employ to be more efficient while working hard.

Step 1: Prioritize

You won't like it but life has a way of throwing things at you willy-nilly and always without your consent. You will have dishes to do, homework to complete, a pipe to fix, and all the while you're just trying to get some actual work done. You may be tempted to leave what really needs to be completed and has a deadline in order to do some other task that's bugging at you. That is, without a doubt, the wrong thing to do. Prioritize, prioritize and prioritize. Make a list if need be and set aside the tasks that can afford to wait a little while longer.

But, of course, it's not always that easy to understand which tasks need more time. You may have multiple projects in equal need of your valuable attention.

Assess everything that needs to be done

Before yanking the breaks off of a project that you've meaning to start, give it a moment's thought and assess it thoroughly. Have you put in enough time to get to know every detail about it? Are you positive that it can be done on time and with the level of accuracy that you strive for? These are real questions that should be on the front of your mind when you're faced with such a situation, especially when you're aware that there are other equally important works to be done.

Make a habit of outlining

You don't necessarily have to use anything digital for this. Just grab a pen and paper and outline it with care. Why? This makes sure you don't repeat a step or more importantly, forget a step. I know that it's hard to understand this point without an example and so here's one - you've been asked to create a website on a certain piece of consumer hardware.

As you may know if you have experience in this field, your first step isn't to code but to design, on paper or otherwise, the basic layout of the website. Once the basics have been put into place, you elaborate on that by creating a wireframe (a mockup of sorts) of it using Photoshop or some other tool. Only when you've absolutely sure that the features that need to be on the website have been accounted for in the final design does the coding bit start.

Most projects can be handle in a similar way. You start from the basics and then you build up from that slowly and steadily.

"No, I'm busy"

You may come off as an inconsiderate individual who only thinks about his own needs but you really need to say no when you're not free. After all, your schedule isn't meant to be screwed with. You must realize that you can't accomplish every single task with the limited amount of time that you've been allotted (unless you're Superman). Therefore, you have every right to turn down additional tasks coming your way, even your own ones!

Avoid Multitasking

It's very easy to claim that you're a multi-tasker, that you can listen to music, answer e-mail and check your WhatsApp all the while doing some work that, in reality, requires your undivided attention. Well, as it happens, your attention does get divided. Your brain gets distracted and you have a hard time staying on the same train of thought, leaving you in a state that's neither efficient nor focused. Yes, it can be argued that music, in particular, can enhance your ability to work but that is not always true in all cases.

Menial tasks can be made better with the help of music as they require less brain power. Something as demanding as, say, programming or financial management cannot be done while you're rocking out. What actually happens when you multitask is that you miss out on everything, or at least half of everything.

You don't get to experience your favorite songs in their fullest not do you get to submit a work that you can be proud of as your heart was in two places at the same time.

Step 2: Learn to deal with the clients the proper way

What constitutes proper communication (and this isn't about etiquette by the way)? How do you handle clients without putting either yourself or your company in a corner? Do you give your client the reins to your horse or do you allow him to be a mere passenger? A smart worker knows how to deal with his clients in a manner that benefits both parties.

Be distinct with your statements

A loose statement such as, "Give me a general idea of what you want. ", is a surefire way of getting yourself into trouble. The client, in most cases, is unsure of what he wants. He came to you for guidance, not the other way around. He wants you, for the most part, to make his decisions for him.

He still has the final say on what he wants but it is your job to narrow down his options. Why? Because you're the guy getting the job done and you know better. While that statement might seem like I'm belittling the client, I'm really not. You see, the client came to you to make use of the services you and your company can provide.

Your company handles more than one project and your client must be told that You will come across clients who will insist that they are running short on time and that they require their work to be done as soon as humanly possible.

You must counter that with the truth – that your company (unless you're a startup) is at any given moment, handling multiple projects and that the turnaround time cannot be pushed forward.

Never take a bad job

Keep in mind that clients are seldom dumb and forgiving. They want to spend as little possible and make the best of that investment. In other words, they're going to squeeze as much out of you as humanly possible and ask you to accomplish tasks that'll really push you to your limits.

Re-bid if necessary

When you take a job, you are given a certain number of
tasks that almost always pertain to your skill level. However,
the wishes of the client may change and he may end up
changing the specifications of the project. In truth, that is
completely normal. Ideas are never set in stone.
They morph with time and it is expected that the changes
will be put into place as they arrive. As you have guessed,
there is a limit to how many times and to what degree you
can change the specifications of a project.
A few changes here and there are fine. But asking a
company to completely redo a project, effectively making it a
new one is anything but acceptable. In those cases, you must
re-bid. Show the client the original project with the original
funding and overlay the new specs on top of that. Tell him
how much more money you'll need to get it done. It is the
client's decision to move ahead with the new bid. Asking the
right questions is by far the smartest thing to do when
dealing with a client.

Step 3: Getting more done faster

Don't be a cheapskate when it comes to maximizing your
work efficiency
In the office, you need proper hardware to get things done.
If you're a programmer developing modern apps, a laptop
from the early 2000s simply won't cut it. Similarly, if you are
a designer and you need a powerful system to render 3D
models as fast as possible, don't go for a mediocre system
that'll groan whenever you open more than two applications
at the same time. Invest on good hardware (and on good
people for that matter) and you'll reap the benefits in the
long run.

How your work matters as much as how long you work

You want to be as efficient as possible – that's a given. But efficiency is hard to maintain when you have a hundred distractions around you. Therefore, make it your mission to make your environment work for you. If you're in an office environment, you probably won't have to worry about that as most offices are quiet places for obvious reasons.

At home though, things can get rowdy. Soundproof your room if need be; do anything that helps you do your work at peace.

A clean working environment also contributes to efficiency. Keep your workspace clean and dust free. You will feel better about yourself and that will help you work faster and efficiently.

Don't shy away from shortcuts

I know what you're thinking, "This book is asking me to take shortcuts?!" Well, by shortcut I don't mean taking the easiest route to a solution, no. What I mean by that is that you can finish everyday tasks faster if you take a moment and figure out which ones are the most repetitive. Checking email every day in the morning is probably the best example when it comes to this. Answering them almost always involves a few select sentences that go with any other email.

So, to make it easier for you and to save time, save your canned responses in a separate document and use them whenever the need calls. Sure, you might have to edit them a bit depending on the context, but the bulk of the work will have been done already!

Give the right person the right job

Not everyone is good at everything. In fact, most people tend to specialize on one thing at a time. Therefore, if you're leading a team, assign your teammates to the right jobs. There's no doubt that you'll see better work get done much faster than before. If you don't know who is best at what, check their resumes and their past work. Better yet, just ask them which project or module they want to handle. They'll gladly tell you all you need to know.

Don't procrastinate if you can help it
Browsing YouTube for hours on end is something that each and every one of us has done in some point of our lives. It's usually a result of working for hours on end and not getting enough rest. Instead of procrastinating and wasting your time on things that bring nothing to the table, go take a walk.

Brew yourself a cup of coffee if you can. Browsing Facebook isn't as rejuvenating as either of those two activities. More importantly, they don't eat up as much of your time. Why? Well, both YouTube and Facebook are endless streams of information. On YouTube, you can move from one video to the next and not even realize that an hour has passed.

It's kind of the same with Facebook. You get notifications from friends and you're tempted to open it and spend time socializing. But you know that it's not helping you earn money and it's certainly not improving your image in the company. So, why not delegate time for entertainment for a later part of your day. Once you get home from work, really put all your attention on TV and web browsing. You'll enjoy it a lot more when you don't have work constantly knocking at your conscience's door.

Accept the fact that you'll never actually be able to maintain your routine

I know how it feels – you set a routine for the day, things go fine up until that moment where you're forced to divert from your original path and do something else. Things like that happen. That's how life goes. So, you must learn how to be flexible with your work. Couldn't get something really important done at the office because you had something else to do? Make time for it at home. Couldn't sleep last night because you had leftover work to do? Go home early, take a nap and continue there. It's hard to make the body break out of its routine but being flexible is really important in this day and age.

Step 4: Take care of your body and your body will take care of you

Proper rest is key to efficiency.

Your body is like an engine. Without proper maintenance, it'll simply fail when you need it the most. Ideally, you should sleep for 8 hours. Any less than that, and your body will deteriorate and that'll really affect your performance at work. Your mind will wear down and you'll find it very hard to concentrate. But why is sleep that important, you ask? Well, our bodies go into repair mode when we sleep. We grow new skin, repair wounds, form memories and a lot more when we sleep. In fact, it's as essential as eating and breathing. The lack of sleep can affect everything you do, not just work. So, if you're reading this book at 3 in the morning, don't. Get yourself to sleep.

Take a break every once in a while

There's nothing wrong with taking short breaks after every hour or so, especially if your work involves staring at the screen all day. When you can, work for 50 minutes and then take a short 10-minute break in which you can go for a walk or just stare out the window (even that can be refreshing (unless you're staring at a brick wall). If you feel ashamed for taking breaks when other around you are still seemingly hard at work, don't worry about it. You're doing your body a favor by letting off the steam.

You need to know your limits
Working yourself to exhaustion isn't what I would call a good day's work. Your body will not like it and your mind will hate you for it. In order to protect your job, you need to protect your body. When you realize that you've worked so hard that the simplest tasks are taking three times longer than usual to finish, you know you've crossed your mental limits. Yes, you must push yourself when you can but it's important to rein yourself back in when you can. After all, your company is depending on you and need to be at your best at all times.

A couple of other things that are worth mentioning
Don't make pay-day "buy everything on your wish list day". Learn to make money for you. Working like a mule and then spending all your hard earned cash is not smart. When you're sick, call it a day and go home. You are obviously not at your 100% when you're suffering from a fever, so don't try and be a hero when you don't need to be. In any case, you'll inevitably be making mistakes at that state, so why bother? Be smart and take rest until you're fully healed.

Don't let time win the race. If you can work, please do. If you have a backlog of tasks that need finishing even though you have time to kill, don't let them stay there. Get them done and you'll thank your past self for being considerate. It's a lot like leaving dishes in the counter after dinner. It's not a terrible idea until they start to stink in the morning.

You'll have to deal with them anyway, so why not do it now when you have ample time?

Chapter 7

The Truth about Self-Motivation

People who are productive and who are also successful don't rely upon others to validate them.
You need to find that motivation inside you. Think how nice it would be to be able to offer someone else in the office a little bit of help. How about being able to go home early and spend more time with the children? You have to see the benefits of your work yourself, rather than depending upon validation from others. This is what gives you incentive and motivation.

When you have a pile of work to do, use the alarm system. Set the alarm for 45 minutes and work solidly during that 45 minutes, knowing that at the end of this time, you can stop and have a walk around and enjoy coffee or your favorite beverage without feeling guilty. When your break is over go back to the timer and set another 45 minutes of solid work during which time you give your attention to the work and nothing else. People around you will get used to you using this system and will respect you when they see just how much you are capable of producing. It's almost like magic.

What you are doing is focusing yourself on one thing during the work time and then giving yourself a break at the end of it. After you have had three 45 minute sessions and are due another break, make this a longer break, such as an hour for lunch. You will have deserved it and you can enjoy sitting down and actually eating your lunch instead of trying to eat a sandwich while you work through your lunch hour. Why it works is because you are setting yourself challenges and working all through the 45 minutes, you achieve that challenge and actually produce more work than you thought you were able to.

The old model of motivation does not work for creative problem solving. Rewarding people with more money, or punishing people based upon a desired outcome only works for mundane, mechanical tasks. Today, thanks to the internet, technology and outsourcing, most of us do not spend time on mechanical, routine tasks. We get paid to be creative, solve problems and invent new ideas, products and services.

So how do you motivate yourself and others to be creative, solve unique challenges, and invent new things? People need intrinsic motivation to perform better at creative tasks, not external motivation. This means they need autonomy, mastery and purpose.

When you have autonomy, you are in control. You decide when you wake up, when you start working, who you work with, where you work, and how you work. With autonomy, you have the freedom to decide what you will work on. This is when you will be at your most creative—when you know you can do anything you want to do without reporting to a superior or having to justify yourself.

Autonomy is important because we can only truly express ourselves and our creativity when we feel in control. People naturally want to be good at what they do. We all want to get better at what we do so we can feel good about ourselves. When you are allowed to master what you do, you will get better results.
When people have the creativity and freedom to do something they enjoy they naturally want to get better at it and develop mastery. As they develop mastery they naturally

find themselves creating new ideas, new solutions and achieving exceptional results.

People want to know that what they do makes a difference in the world. People want to be a part of something bigger than themselves.

Everyone wants to contribute to others. It's just human nature. When we embrace this and allow ourselves and others to develop their own sense of purpose and understand why what we do makes a difference, our results will improve dramatically.

If you're not feeling motivated to take action and improve your life, take a look at your autonomy, mastery and purpose. When you have all three aligned, motivation will come from within, and you won't need someone else telling you what to do to improve your life. You'll do it naturally because it's what you want to do.

Believing you can

Have you ever wondered why some people achieve their goals while others fail? Here is the secret: the successful ones made it a must. They are committed to making it happen. They didn't 'hope' it would happen; they didn't wish for it to happen; they didn't think, "It would be nice if it happened." No, they decided it will happen.

What about you? Are you committed to creating your ideal career or are you merely interested?

If you're merely "interested," you'll try making changes in your life for a few months, and when things don't work out as planned you'll give up. But when you're totally committed, you'll do whatever it takes to make it happen. You won't give up until you achieve the results you really want. It might take more time than you thought—it usually does—but you will eventually generate the results you want.

In short, if you're interested, you'll probably fail, but if you're committed, you'll likely succeed.

The act of committing may not sound very practical to you, but it is one of the most practical things you can do. Committing—like believing—is using the invisible (your mind) to create the visible (an exciting career).

Pain & Pleasure

You are driven by these two twin forces and this will help you understand why a human being doesn't want to change or take action towards their dreams. How to motivate a human being even if they don't want to change.

You can start understanding what human psychology is and why it is so hard for someone to move forward. Why is the majority of the world overweight? Answer is because they associate pleasure to eating chocolate and cakes. A smoker smokes cigarettes because he knows in the future it will have a massive effect on his health which is pain. The problem is the pain is way off in the future and the pleasure of the cigarette is right now.

The only way to change habits like this is to give the client intense, unbearable and immediate levels of pain. Let's say the smoker has a heart attack, that's immediate pain and most of the time they will stop that habit. There are some cases that they still smoke but most of the time a shock like that will make them stop. A strategy for creating change with people is getting them to associate massive amounts of pain to their present behavior or pattern they keep running.

There is a way of doing this but it's up to you to get the client into the state, they will have to experience a lot of momentary pain. It's all about getting yourself to go into the future and feel, hear and see what you will look like if you keep going down this road.

This technique isn't about thinking about it but feeling it. A smoker isn't going to change a habit if they think about what could happen but a deep gut painful experience in your nervous system will change and open up a way of thinking. Your brain will do anything to avoid pain and if we can use it to our advantage then, you will rapidly change any habit or emotion you want.

Some of the things we do to ourselves hurt us and we even know we are doing it to ourselves but we honestly believe we can't break out. Most people live their life this way and have the pleaser mentality.

Clearing limiting beliefs

1. Write down all the limiting beliefs that are not serving you.
2. Once you've done this, pick one at a time. The most effective way to clear this once and for all is to get your brain to associate massive immediate pain to this belief. You must feel deep in your gut that not only has this belief cost you pain in your past, but it's costing you pain in the present and ultimately, can bring you pain in your future.
3. After you have associated immediate pain to that belief, your brain will be in the position to do anything to change so then you must associate tremendous pleasure to adopting a new empowering belief to take its place.
4. Remember, if you clear your limiting beliefs, your life will free up more than anything you do. Remember that it's really important to actually feel the pain for a short five to ten minutes and do whatever it takes. The short period of pain for a lifetime of freedom is worth it.

After you have cleared your limiting beliefs and reframed your old beliefs to positive new beliefs, the integration starts to take place.

What do you really want?

What do you want to do for a living? How much money do you want to make? Where do you want to live? How many days to you want to work per week? How many hours? Do you want long vacations? If so, how long? What does your ideal day look like? At what time do you want to wake up? What skills do you want to develop? What emotions do you want to experience more of? What does your 'best self' look like? What's the deadline by which you must achieve this vision? When will you start?

Finding out what you love

Do you know what you love? Can you clearly articulate your passions? If not, the exercises in this section will help. To uncover your true passions, let's start by gathering some valuable clues. More specifically, we will look at the following:
Twenty things you love the most
What you focus on and think about most often
What you prefer to do in your spare time
What your feelings say about your passions
What you can learn from past experiences
What you envision for yourself, (your dreams)
What your intuition tells you, and
How other people see you and what you can learn from this. The purpose of this exercise is to start brainstorming potential career ideas based on the top five things you love the most. Don't hold back, welcome even the silliest ideas. Forget about the practicality of your ideas or even whether or not you have any interest in pursuing them. Just come up with as many ideas as you can. Because your perspective is limited, you might want to ask your family and friends to join you. You're likely to come up with more ideas this way.

You can learn a lot by observing your emotions. While negative emotions signal your need to change something, feelings of joy, passion and excitement indicate that you're on the right path. The question you need to ask yourself is, how do I experience more of that joy and passion in my life? How can I design my life in such a way that I'm living to a purpose?

Developing 'I Will' Mindset

Adopting an 'I Will' Mindset means you develop a long-term perspective and fully understand the power of patience. As a result, you avoid common traps and manage to remain motivated long-term until you finally achieve your career goal.

Misjudging the amount of time and effort needed
In general, people are terrible at planning. They tend to be overly optimistic regarding what they can accomplish short-term, while underestimating what they can accomplish long-term. As a consequence, they are prone to giving up before reaping the fruits of their efforts.

Underestimating the power of perseverance

People tend to give too much importance to external factors such as talent or luck, failing to realize that with enough effort and persistence their goals are possible. They underestimate what they are truly capable of doing and forget the most important thing: they can always learn, grow and improve. As a result of this underestimation, they become impatient when they don't achieve their goals. Or, worse, they stop improving, believing they've reached their limits. This is seldom the case. More often than not, their approach is the problem. By putting in place a different type

of practice and reflecting on their performance weekly or
even daily, they will improve.

Overly focusing on the results

By learning to focus on the process—what you do every day—
rather than on the results—the target you set—you will
dramatically increase the chance of achieving your goals in
the long run.

For instance, let's say you want to lose weight. A result goal
would be to lose twenty pounds by the end of the year. A
process goal would be to eat a certain type of food and to
exercise on a consistent basis. There is no guarantee you will
lose twenty pounds, but if you follow the process every day,
over the long term you will generate good results and will
likely achieve your goals—even if it takes more time than you
thought.

Once you commit to changing your career, be willing to
spend a few years until you end up exactly where you want to
be. That's a normal process. Every successful individual
knows it requires tons of effort and a lot of patience to make
significant changes in one's life. Do not give up before you
reach your target. Hang in on there.

Give yourself enough time to change your career. Set a clear
deadline, two to three years from now, (this may take longer
depending on how challenging your career goal happens to
be). Then, make a promise to yourself you will never quit
before this deadline. If you do so, you'll be astonished by
what you can accomplish in just a few years.

Chapter 8

Finding the essence of your goal

You need to have clear ideas of what your goals are. This could mean goals for the day, goals for the week, the month or the year. When you ask someone who was not productive about what he intended to achieve this week, he will be so stressed out that he could not give you an answer. He had allowed work to pile up to such an extent that the task became enormous.

Why it's necessary to have goals, even small ones, is so that you achieve and can feel good about your achievements. Of course, things may get in the way occasionally but that's normal too. These are called hurdles and everyone experiences them. The way that you minimize hurdles is what matters or the way that you use mistakes to learn from and then move on in a positive way.

It sounds very simple when it's said like that, but it really can work like that. Don't be a perfectionist and spend all of your time on detailed listing. Don't be afraid of your own failure and not even try. Both of these failing will stop you from every achieving and people don't know it, but often their own psychological workings are what stands in the way of success. Why make things more complex than they need to be? Why be afraid of failure when you haven't even started your tasks yet?

Write down in a notebook what you want to achieve in your life. Close your eyes for a moment and be the success that you always wanted to be. To be successful and productive you have to think like people who are successful and productive. Thus, you need to set your mindset to success, rather than sit on your laurels and believe that success happens to everyone else except you.

When you make goals that are not attainable or try to push yourself further than hours permit, what you end up with is disappointment. Thus, you need to be able to triage your work and decide upon the following:

What work can wait or is low priority?

What work needs your full attention and is relatively urgent?

What work can you give to someone else?

When you know what work needs to be done within the next 24 hours, you may look at your list and despair because it's all too much for you. However, there's a very good way to deal with it once you have sorted out what you can achieve in the next 24 hours. The work that is routine and non-urgent can be put to one side for the morning tomorrow. The work that you can delegate to someone else shows trust in another member of staff. Stop being the martyr when you know that others can do certain tasks better than you can. Let them. If you empower other people, you show your ability to manage and that's why some people get promoted quicker than others. It isn't about YOU doing all the work yourself.

Now create the list of the urgent work and if this still seems hard, split large jobs into smaller and more manageable portions, so that each of these parts of the job can be considered as goals. What you are doing is making your goals more manageable and that's what helps you when you are trying to be productive. When you see success, albeit small in the first couple of days, this gives you the motivation to do better and you will find that you will actually achieve much more than you ever did before. Challenging yourself is a good thing, though in the early days of giving yourself lists, make the lists doable so that you have the incentive to succeed in the future and then make the lists a little harder so that you have to work to achieve them. This increases your level of satisfaction and also your production rate. Although it's great to have big dreams, it's important to recognize that you aren't going to get there in a single day, it is likely to take months and probably years to achieve them. So how to keep yourself motivated when you are on such a long journey? We obviously you have to enjoy the journey or it will be such a hard slog that even if you do manage to stick with it, you may wonder if it was worthwhile. But equally, you will need to set yourself intermediate goals, to break it down into smaller bite-sized chunks.

If your goal is to run a marathon, then unless you are starting from a really high level of fitness, then you are going to need months to prepare your body to survive the ordeal in good shape. You are going to have to build up to running that distance by starting out running for shorter distances and building up gradually. Each time you achieve a longer distance on one of your long runs, that's another milestone on your journey. But even these intermediate targets are not enough. Many runners set themselves weekly mileage targets, but I believe that quality is more important than quantity, so set yourself the target of achieving several key sessions each week and to focus on making each of these a really good quality session, rather than running lots of miles with no particular aim.

Integrating your goal into your life

The next step is to make your goal part of your life. Do you often complain because you have insufficient time left to do what you love? Well, you will have to find the time. When you're serious about your goal, you will make the time for whatever you're committed to.
The best way to make a living doing what you love is simply by starting to do what you love. How else could you do it?

Perhaps, you have a busy schedule and believe you cannot find the time. If this is the case, start small. Dedicate five or ten minutes to your goal each day. Over time you will build momentum and will naturally want to do more of the same. There are several ways to work on your goal. I believe the best approach is to dedicate time to it first thing in the morning. Learn to prioritize. Whatever's most important to you, do it first. Otherwise, as the day gets busy, you risk forgetting about it and lose momentum.

At the beginning of each week block chunks of time to focus on your goal. Make sure you schedule them in a calendar or a notebook. If you can't work on your goal first thing in the morning, do it as soon as you finish work and/or during the weekend. You can also use your lunch break.

Creating an action plan

To turn your goal into reality you need to put a specific action plan in place. For now, let's focus on your major career goal. If you would like to pursue several goals simultaneously, simply repeat the following process for each one.

The first step is to write down all the tasks you need to complete to achieve your goal. Include everything you can think of. Focus on the big picture and identify the key milestones you must go through to attain your ultimate goal. If you don't know all the tasks your goal involves, do your research. Start by searching for general articles on how to achieve your goal. This will give you the big picture. Whenever possible, talk to people who have the career you want. It will cut through the noise, saving you a lot of time and effort. Simply ask them what you need to do to build a similar career.

Setting goals

Now you have created a plan, let's write down more specific goals. I recommend you break your long-term goal into yearly, quarterly, monthly, weekly and daily goals.

To set goals, we'll simply use the milestones you already put in your plan. For daily and weekly goals select the tasks you've written down and assign them to a specific week. If needed, break these tasks down even further.

I understand that if you have never set written goals before, it may sound overwhelming. Don't worry though. Start by setting yearly, quarterly and monthly goals based on your milestones. You'll find that weekly and daily goals come naturally. All you have to do is to break down your larger goals into smaller ones.

Setting weekly goals

To set weekly goals, ask yourself, what could you accomplish this week, to make it a great week? What would really move the needle forward? Try to aim for three to six goals.

Setting daily goals

To set daily goals look at your list of weekly goals and further break them down whenever relevant. Add other tasks you want to complete that day if needed. Again, aim at three to six daily goals, and this includes your Key Success Factors.

The most effective way to set daily goals is to plan your day the previous night. Before going to bed, make it a habit to spend a few minutes to think of what you want to accomplish the next day, and create a list. Alternatively, you can plan your day first thing in the morning. This habit alone will boost your productivity and significantly increase your chances of reaching your goal.

To write down your goals you can use a simple notebook or an agenda. No need for fancy tools. Just use a new page each day to write your daily goals. You can also use the template in your action guide.

Building Accountability

Are you committed to achieving your goal? If so, putting in place an accountability system will further help you reach your commitments in the long-term.

We tend to take more action and move faster when we have someone who keeps us accountable. This is one of the roles performed by a coach for instance. If you want to maximize your chances of success, you must have some sort of accountability.

To know whether you have such a system right now, simply ask yourself, who will call me out if I don't do what I said I would do? If the answer is nobody, then you don't have an effective or reliable accountability system.

Chapter 9

Your Relationship with Money

To keep track of your wealth, have a take at the following. First, money is more than just that, money it is part of your entire life. Do everything with one heart especially for the business owners. Do not be a passive visitor to your company place of investment. The more involved you are with your source of money, the more easily it will get when handling anything money. Money is a sign that you are changing the world. Know what you want and exactly why you may want it and go for it. Know the limits of the things that are possible. Love the money and have a positive attitude toward the flow of income. Do not have negative thoughts about investing and money. Yes, there are lots of things that were nasty and untrue that many parents say about money, but it is good to ignore such as their opinions are not informed. Many negative comments are out of frustration and are not sincere in any way. Build positive energy that will keep you on the path to financial freedom. Do not be emotional about spending. Rational thought is a big plus in money matters. Make sure the decisions made are not based on the slumps of the stock market, or the prices and rates of the mortgage interest. Keep hands off the savings. One of the most efficient ways of saving up for some future goals is to save money and forget about it. Do not hole up any hope in the cash that has accumulated along the way. Keep the savings untouched.

Finally, it will be awesome to make money a friend not an enemy. Let money work for you, do not allow yourself to work out to the point of death. Keep the right work ethics but make sure there is a small allowance to rest, rethinking and strategizing. Remember to stay focused on the things that will actually build your resolve to work smart.

Chapter 10

The Debt Free Mindset

Being debt-free does not mean not having debts. It simply means changing your mindset about your debts and using the latter wisely to obtain the things you need and want. Learn how you can acquire a debt-free mindset and have a better financial edge over someone who doesn't.

Changing Your Debt Outlook
Accept the fact that changing your mindset can take a while. This is the first step to having the mindset of being debt-free. Changing the way, you view and treat debts is something that can take more than one day to happen. However, once the change does take place, you will find yourself progressing faster than you can imagine.
Stop treating debt as a way to buy things. Like most people, you may be likely to view the practice of taking on debt as a normal activity. However, you have to stop thinking of loan applications and credit payments as a regular method of getting the things you want.
Know how to separate the good debts from the bad ones. All types of debt carry risks, but there are good debts that you can maximize in order to financially empower you instead.

Harnessing the Power of Credit

Once you have changed your mindset, you can apply the following tips on using your debts to your advantage.
Make use of debts to build good credit. Taking on debt is actually a good way of improving your credit standing, as long as you make sure to pay off the debt on time. Don't

wait for the interest attached to it to pile up; take steps to pay back your debt as soon as you can.

Take advantage of several debt benefits. You also have to realize that debt is actually a fast way for you buy the things you need. You won't be affected when buying in business establishments that do not accept personal checks since you can simply use a credit card, which is accepted anywhere. Taking on debt is also a way of letting you afford expensive necessities, such as a house. The important thing to remember is to pay off the monthly payments on schedule.

Money Management

Having a good system for organizing your bills goes a long way to affect your finances positively. Case in point, you can without much of a stretch, pay them on time rather than defaulting. Additionally, the simplicity of discovering them out will help you resolve issues concerning payments as well. The primary step is to get a monthly planner for every year beginning from the current one. Register the dates of bill payments and spot them side by side with your payday. Keep the bills to be paid in your planner and discover with repeating bill ought to be shouldered. Verify the bill with the closest payment date is continue top of the second one. Check the bill again for rightness. Make no space for a lot of paperwork that goes hand in hand with a bill. Let the whip can contain them and not your document. Set out at any rate once a month, a period to sort out your bills. Give a different planner to repeating bills and an alternate for different charges every month. A decent practice is to write on the planner the name and due date of the bill. At the point when the invoice comes, write on it the check number, sum paid and the date it was paid before conferring it to filing. After bills have been paid, attempt to file them promptly into their different envelopes. Additionally, organize the envelopes consecutively for simplicity of recovery. All scratched off checks you have must be domiciled in a specific folder in company of the statements of the bank. Next is to print the dates onto the envelope. You might additionally need to make an alternate planner for bank statements and for income taxes. When things like doctor's visit expenses and real property tax bills are paid [these bills can be deducted on your tax returns], keep them documented in "For income taxes" rather than paid bills document. For every year, begin another planner system and an alternate box for putting away those as well. Doing this normally has a lot more advantages for you. Case in point, it helps you stay informed concerning your using propensities. The underhanded over use is principally awful when you are not keeping records. Also, you will have the capacity to focus your cash inflow and outflow. This will help you in the event that you need to undertake a new project. You have to first tally the expense to know whether your present financial status can convey the weight or not.

Chapter 11

Creating Financial Independence and Real Economic Freedom

Financial independence is freedom. It is the ability to do what you want, when you want, without worrying about paying your bills or having to work to continue to support yourself and your family. Financial independence is both a state of mind and a reality based upon your financial situation.

To be financially independent, your passive income (cash inflow) must exceed your expenses (cash outflow).

Why is Passive Income Important?

Passive income means that you do not have to work to continue to bring in income. With enough passive income, you could literally sit on the beach and party the rest of your life and not worry about money ever again.

Now, that is a bit of an exaggeration because there will always be some management you will have to do with any business or passive income source. If one of your passive income sources is real estate, you're going to have to manage your real estate properties (or at least manage the person who you've hired to manage your real estate for you).

There's always going to be SOME work to do if you want to MAINTAIN and grow your income. But it doesn't have to be much.

Financial independence gives you the time and the resources to truly make a difference with your life instead of just trying to get by. True abundance comes when you have financial independence, and the entire world benefits when you get rich.

Chapter 12

Steps to Erase Debt by Changing Your Habits

Removing debt is actually about changing your habits. Bad cash behaviors are the reasons that have gotten you to the economic chaos that you will be in now. You should recognize these practices and modify them. Listed below are 4 Steps by Changing Your Practices to Erase Debt.

Identify Your Bad Habits

So what are your bad debt practices? It may be you are poor using the paperwork. Not checking the amount of money venturing out and coming in. Not managing your checkbook could fall under this class.
It might be eating dinner too often out at restaurants. Whatever it is, recognize your bad habits.

Write It Down

See if your habits are currently showing up in your budget. If they're not easily identifiable within your budget worksheets separate out these charges, so they are better to see. It might be you have a "miscellaneous" group or line-item where these expenses disappear into. You'll split them out to their line items so that it is not difficult to recognize them and change them.

Adjust Your Allowance

Next, modify your allowance, which is also your strategy, so that you consider that income that was likely to these poor practices and redirect them to a different cost, ultimately debt repayment. Or should you be in continuous overdraft then these recognized styles of spending may be your admission to obtain out of the debt trap? Simply use that money to fund your important costs, like food housing, and utilities, to avoid more spending. If there is any left, then throw it at the debt settlement to accelerate that.

Kill Your Bad Habits

This may likely be the hardest part. You will quit by not participating in them. Having an operating budget will reprogram your mind. But sometimes simply taking a poor habit away enables you to require it more. To overcome the habit try replacing it with a good routine. Or even a better routine.
Debt may be the result of habits. Understanding how to recognize them, then killing these problems, adjusting your budget and publishing them along can help you build success and continue to eliminate debt.
 Getting into debt and having bad credit scores tend to be the result of weak financial practices. Thus, it's critical that you start cultivating superior economic habits as early as possible. Listed below are three of them as you can begin learning immediately:

Learn to budget

Overspending causes many debt issues. This is the place where a budget might help. You can be told by a budget how much you should be shelling out for each product in your life. This enables your financial life to remain organized. You ought to begin to list most of the charges you've down. Including book, tools, food, personal care, travel, spending cash, amusement, passions, and training, along with other things.

Then verify full spending against your income. If your earnings cannot help it or you rarely manage, you have to cut down on your costs.

You ought not to commit away from budget except if it is an urgent situation while a budget ought to be flexible.

Live within your means

If you should be getting $40k a year but have unpaid payments and extreme debt, it's time to improve your lifestyle. Numerous people have a very good credit rating and extremely small debt.

The easiest way to make sure that you have a superb credit rating - regardless of what your income - is always to invest less than you generate. That means living below your means. When you have a very little money, you will need to reside with roommates so that you can keep down costs. If you have a medium sized income, that will imply saving more and engaging less.

Your earnings isn't a factor in identifying your credit rating but the method you control income, and your debts do. Even though you today in case you acquire the lottery, your credit rating would not be damaged. Remember, it is how you manage your cash that issue.

Save and Spend

Saving is one of the most efficient methods to make sure your credit score keeps in prime condition. It is because you will be prepared for financial problems and your money may grow. In case you have the practice of saving and reinvesting, it is unlikely you'll enter into the bad behavior of overspending. Damage to your credit score is very much reduced and your chance of stepping into debt.

You must get information on money management to enhance your knowledge. There are various easy and positive economic behaviors you can add into your daily life. The faster you do it, the easier your daily life is going to be.

Chapter 13

Manage Your Money like a Rich Person

When the subject of managing money comes up, most people think, "I don't have much money, why do I need to learn how to manage it?" The truth of the matter is that, if you managed your money better, you'd have more money! If you are broke, you can become financially free in a short period of time.

Some people think that money isn't important. I mean, it's certainly not as important as your health, love or happiness, is it? This is a very harmful and self-sabotaging belief that most people carry around unconsciously.

Let me ask you a question...

If you told your wife she wasn't important, would she stick around very long?

If you told your husband he wasn't important, would he stay with you?

If you told your friends they weren't important, would they introduce you to more friends?

The answer to these questions is, "of course not!"

Likewise, if you believe money is not important, it won't stick around. It will leave you. And it will never work for you to bring in more and more money.

Financially successful people understand that money is very important in the areas that money is important in. Have you ever tried to buy a house with a down payment of love and monthly installments of happiness? I don't think most bankers would accept that deal.

If you want to buy a house, clothes, food, entertainment, toys, games, trips, electronics, electricity, gas, utilities and other goods, and invest in businesses, and organizations, and give to charity, you're simply going to need money.

So money is very important when it comes to buying these things. Love is not as important as money when it comes to buying these things. In your relationships, love is, of course, more important than money. But so what? That's how it should be.

Always remember: money is very important in the areas that money is important in. Let go of any other limiting beliefs around money.

Chapter 14

How Budgeting Helps You Meet Your Goals

Budgeting is an important step in helping you meet your goals. Budgeting isn't just about being careful with your money. You can use budgeting tools to help you plan your income and spending so that you can intentionally set aside savings. You can use expense tracking to help you trim the fat from your budget and see where you can make changes to improve your overall quality of life, now and in the future. Your long term financial goals, as well as your short term way of life, can only be realized through effective budgeting. There are three primary ways to budget. You can budget by week or pay period, month, or by expense. Budgeting by expense is the easiest way to budget. It is generally done by using the envelope method, which will be explained shortly. Budgeting by week or pay period can help you stop the paycheck to paycheck cycle, but works with that mentality while you work to improve your financial habits. Monthly budgeting is helpful because you can see everything you spend monthly at one time. This is important because many bills are only paid once per month.

You may choose to use a combination of methods. Sometimes it can be helpful to have even the most basic monthly budget to use in combination with a weekly budget. It can also help to use the envelope method, especially if you have difficulty setting aside money for larger expenses. Regardless of what method you use to budget, you will need to understand some basic concepts that must be used. These tools and concepts are vitally important to your budgeting success. They should be used diligently, especially when you are just starting out. You will need to use the information from these tools to help you create effective and accurate budgets.

Tracking Income

There are some important things to keep in mind when tracking income. You want your budget to be as accurate as possible. If you overestimate how much income you will have you could throw your entire budget off balance. You could wind up short for the week or month, and be unable to pay an important bill. When you consider your income for your budget you should calculate all reliable sources of income. This means that you need to incorporate only that income which is guaranteed. This is usually your paycheck. When you calculate the money you will have, don't use your gross pay. If you work the same number of hours per week you can use the net pay from your check stubs to see what you can budget for income. If your work hours vary, calculate your gross income and deduct 25% for taxes. You may have fewer deductions than that, but it is better to be safe than sorry. You may have other sources of income such as that from a side job, child support or alimony. If you have steady income from one or more of these sources that is guaranteed, feel free to add it to your budgeted income. Guaranteed income is income that is received on a scheduled basis. It also must be received with continuity, such as on time each period for at least three to six months. If you have a child support or alimony order but the money doesn't always come on time or at all, you should not count it as income in your budget. If you budget for this income and then it doesn't show up it will throw your entire financial plan out of whack and you will have to face potentially serious consequences.

Tracking Expenses

There are many ways that you can track your expenses and spending. Tracking expenses is especially important when you first start budgeting. It is vital that you know where all of your money is going. Creating a budget of what you anticipate spending is an important aspect of your budget. But tracking expenses tells you where your money is actually going. Tracking expenses is important because it helps you determine what you need to budget for. Bills like rent and a car payment are fixed expenses that you don't really have to think about. But most expenses are variable, meaning that they are different each month. The only way to budget for variable expenses is to have some idea of what that amount might be. It is pretty easy to track your expenses. You can easily create a spreadsheet on your computer where you can enter your expenses daily and have a monthly total running at the bottom. There are such spreadsheets available online as well. This requires keeping receipts and entering each expense. You can also get expense trackers on your smart phone with many different available apps. This is helpful for making sure that you don't miss any expenses when you enter them into your tracking at home. If you are single you can just use the expense tracker app. If you have a significant other, you will need to combine your tracking and theirs on a master spreadsheet or software.

Budgeting for Variable Expenses

This is where your expense tracker will come in handy. When you track your spending for the previous month you can use that information to help you budget for your variable expenses for the following month. As you continue this trend you can calculate the average spending for that item based on several months of data. This will give you the most accurate budget possible.

It is important that you give yourself some leeway when it comes to variable expenses. You should always pad them, even if just by a few dollars, when doing your budget. This way you will not run into serious problems if the expense ends up being a bit more than you thought. If you have extra money at the end of the budget period because you padded your variable expenses you can use that money to help make larger purchases that you couldn't afford before, or you can add it to your savings nest egg.

It is best to budget as closely as possible. As already mentioned your expense tracker can help you with some of that. Past spending habits can help you calculate the budget for things like gasoline, food and household items. Some variable expenses require a different tactic.

Gauging Success

The first thing you will notice when this budget is working properly is that you never run out of money before the next payday. You will always be able to cover everything you need to, and without being completely broke. Even if you have only a few dollars left when that next check hits, you have accomplished keeping yourself from overspending, and you are likely living within your means. Hopefully you are managing to build up a nest egg as well.

The second thing you will notice when you use this budget wisely is that your monthly bills are paid—and it doesn't seem like a hardship. When you try to pay your rent out of one check you can feel like you don't even have enough money to eat. But when you break up that rent payment over multiple pay periods, you feel like you can breathe. It is much less stressful to budget for bills in this fashion.

Finally, when this budget is being used properly you will discover that you have more money than you thought you did. If you stick to the budget you make you will be able to easily afford everything you need, and perhaps some things that you want.

Chapter 15

Saving Money

Savings are for the long term so one will need a hard line standing against present pressures to spend extravagantly, in exchange for a dignified future full of great investments. Certified financial planners will confirm that the resolve to accumulate money contrary to the normal spending is a huge stepping stone towards the realization of successful savings plans. Savings are often contentious and vary in effect from person to person. However, the best method to know how much one will be comfortable with is probably to set a fixed percentage of savings to set aside each year.

When you start to become creative in how you can buy the things you still want and need for a smaller amount, you will want to put the money you are saving into your bank savings account.

Everybody knows that for every income there must be a saving culture involved for wealth to be created. A typical worker will be placed like thus: They have a job and earning some substantial amount of income. Again, probably there is a family in the picture. Another possibility is that the worker probably doesn't have a family but wants the best for the future defendants. All these scenarios depict possible situations that are encountered in everyday and call for careful planning for the finances. Many investors will need to have clear picture of what exactly they want and what is required of them. This must obviously be in line to their dreams and rhyme with the current financial situation.

Be focused on a particular goal. Do not be general as this will give room for complacency.

As a way of making sure you are on the right track, take a break once in a while and monitor the progress. For every five or so months, keep a keen eye on the growth of your finances and stay focused on making the best of every opportunity. It will be very vital to do a thorough analysis of the growth advanced and make the best decisions on growing the fund. If you have better working alternatives, do not switch at once, try with a thin proportion of monies and when successful, scale slowly but do not exceed. The more mature your portfolio gets, the better your chances for reaping huge rewards.

When you start saving stick to your goals. Do not waver at the choice of what exactly you want. Be familiar with your retirement needs. It is very important to keep on psyching yourself using other methods such as attending seminars or just networking with friends. Whatever you do, keep focused.

Chapter 16

Taking Action. Starting Investing

Collecting Capital

The first task when investing is knowing where you will get your capital. Most people use their own money to start. This is necessary for some investment activities like investing in securities. Ideally, you should use cash for securities, and there is no better source of cash than your own savings. Loans are perfectly acceptable for some types of investments. This is particularly useful if you choose to invest in real estate properties or if you choose to set up and start your own business.

You can also collect money from other investors who may be willing to put money on your proposed ventures. To get capital this way, you will need to approach potential investors and pitch them your plan for investing in real estate, or for putting up your own business.

In major investing cities like New York, London and Toronto, you will find many people who have the cash to fund your business ventures. It's just a matter of convincing them that your investment plan will work, and will be worth investing on.

Even if you are not in these cities though, you can still approach other people to fund your plans.

For instance, you can start with interested friends and family members. You can also make use of the power of the internet through crowd sourcing. America is the leading country when it comes to outsourcing startups. Many people are looking for ideas to fund.

Just like with individual investors, you just have to create a package to offer the crowd for them to start investing in your ideas.

Connect with the Right Professionals

After collecting the necessary capital for your investment, the next step is to gather your team.

In most types of investments, you will not be able to do it alone. You will either need to work with a professional in the field that you wish to participate in or work with a service that will facilitate for you.

In real estate for example, you usually need to work with a real estate broker. This professional is licensed to promote and facilitate the sale of your property.

If you are flipping properties, you may also need to work with people who will help you make repairs and do property feature upgrades, depending on what the property needs to increase its value.

If you are planning to start investing in securities, on the other hand, you will need to work with the right broker or investing service.

In the stock market, for instance, you will need to work with stock brokers. These people are licensed to facilitate the buying and selling of company stocks listed in the stock exchange.

They can also give you some expert advice on how to invest, and which stocks to buy or sell.

If you are planning to put your money into managed accounts or automated investment funds like the index fund, you will need to connect with the right investment fund company.

These companies make the investment process for you. Usually, they are easy to contact and you can visit them in their offices. They usually have an office conveniently located near the areas they are operating in.

These firms are also the leading providers of online services in the industry. They provide you with a way to invest in the assets they offer even if you cannot physically go to their office.

In this case, you may be required to provide documentation as proof of your identity and income.

These are required by law to make sure that your sources of income are legitimate and that you are not laundering other people's money.

Design Your Own Investing Strategy

Now that you have the right professionals in your corner, you can now start investing.

Regardless of the type of asset that you have selected to put your funds in, you still need to make other important decisions.

When investing in the stock market, for instance, you will need to make the decision of which companies, sector or index to invest in.

You also need to plan how long you will hold the asset and how much of your funds you will commit to that asset.

In the real estate market, on the other hand, you will need to decide on whether you want to buy a residential or a business property. You also need to make a plan on how you are going to make money with it. Are you going to rent it out or sell it for a profit?

These decisions are crucial to make sure that you make a profit in all of your investment activities. Without a clear plan from the beginning, you will end up making rushed decisions that may lead to losses.

Remember to stick to your target amount for funds that are committed to specific life goals. Once you reach your target amount, you should force yourself to liquidate the assets and withdraw your money.

Chapter 17

Tips to work less and earn more

Do your 'own' job

Do your work. There's plenty of work to do when you are a manager and if you keep delegating it then you might come to realize that some of it keeps piling up over time, simply because the employees you have designated the specific tasks to are not quite all that capable of doing the same. Allocate what you feel can be done best by yourself, like trying to 'close' an all too important client yourself, and you will come to realize that your work has been done with an all too superior efficacy. Your employees will look up to you as well and perhaps even get a dollop of inspiration from the way you have gone about closing that 'big' client, causing them to strive towards closing their own clients, working harder towards the presentations they are making, having gotten that extra boost they need by seeing 'you', their 'boss', having gone out there in the 'market' as well just like they do every single day. There's no better way to make your employees work than to do work yourself. It creates a healthy atmosphere that always produces the desired effects. So get out of that chair and go out there and do your bit. That's the least you can do if you want to start being a better manager!

Be 'Real'

Often we assume different personas at work and altogether different ones at the workplace. For instance, you might really be a very kind, gentle and soft person in reality, something probably only your wife and kids know, but in the office you might put on your 'Mr. Hyde' persona and scare the living daylights out of your employees. Think about it. Is it really worth all the effort to alter your personality so dramatically on a day-to-day basis? After all, you're no actor in Hollywood going to the studio every morning and playing a character that is far removed from his or her skin. Have you ever considered the fact that being 'gentle' and 'soft' in the workplace might really work wonders for you, as opposed to the brash and abrasive personality you have adopted to 'suit' the needs at your workplace? The thing is, people resonate well with you if you are your true self with them. If you're being somebody you're not, you're really not going to be all that effective in your communication skills. Also, it's not what being a 'human being' is all about. Being human is really all about talking to people and sharing your personal life with them as well as taking a real interest in their personal lives. This gives them a feeling of being valued and being seen for who they truly are, just like they would like to see 'you' for that which you really are. This will facilitate better communication between you and your employees, and it will ensure that things don't fall out of plan simply because there was a glaring lack of communication. After all, the more 'real' you are with your employees, the more 'approachable' you will be, really, and that will go a long way in ensuring that there is superior communication between you and your employees, as well as keeping them high on the fact that their boss is really a 'human being', after all. A win-win situation, really!

Self-Awareness

No, this is not the kind of self-awareness that the Buddha attained when meditating under that tree so many years ago. Perhaps it might be a long-term aspiration of yours, but let's focus on the matter at hand here, which is really being 'aware' of the way you are reacting at work. Think about it. You might have really started the day on a wrong footing. Your wife had a major fight with you in the morning and stormed out of the house. Her phone is switched off as you try her desperately on the way to work and she won't respond to your messages. So what do you do? Why you take it out on your team in the boardroom in the morning, of course, for no fault of theirs. There's that all too old adage that says that you should 'Never mix business with pleasure.' Well, there's time for a new one now as well. 'Never mix pain with pleasure' as well. Because you might end up saying something nasty to your employees in a bout of frustration, something you might really regret later. Watch yourself constantly. Are you being snappish all the time? Is it because of something in your personal life that is bothering you? You're busy firing your employee because he hasn't shaved this morning, but have you given a thought as to how you are reacting yourself at the workplace? The way your wife has reacted this morning has only gone to sour your mood to a great extent and what you are doing with your employee right now is just that. Perhaps your wife really had probable cause to behave the way she did, but you most certainly don't. The chances that the employee you just yelled at is going to go ahead and muck up his day are increased manifold, all for no fault of theirs! They will feel that they have messed up in their work, only causing them to employ a negative attitude henceforth. And we all know just how much negativity can hinder productivity. So that is something we most certainly don't want. If you're really having a bad day, take a few moments to sit back and take a deep breath. Thinking about your problem at home is not going to make it any better. In fact, you're only making it worse. What's more, your problem at home will be compounded if you let it affect your behavior at work, because its negative effect will most certainly trickle down to your workforce as well. So just sit back and relax for a few moments and tell yourself that there is a time when you can deal with that problem of yours, and that is later. Your bad mood at work might just be the reason he walks out of that office without sealing that deal after all. You want to foster a spirit of positivity at work, and that begins with the way you feel and behave. So be aware of how you feel and react at all times and you will be surprised at just how easy it is to get a hold on yourself before things spiral and go out of control!

Fun! Fun! Fun!

Sure, that's what life is all about, isn't it? Especially to a two year old, that is. When we grow up we make the mistake of getting too serious about our lives. We get jobs and work our way up the rungs of promotion, not giving a thought to the fact that the whole process should really be 'fun', after all. And what fun is there without friends? If you don't treat your employees like your 'friends' then you will ensure that they too are deprived of the 'fun' that can really go a long way in bolstering productivity!

Think about it. There's a reason they said 'All work and no play makes Jack a dull boy'. That's because it's integral that we have fun every single day of our lives. And of course, nobody says that you have to 'Mix business with pleasure.' You can schedule the pleasurable activities after your work hours, but with the people who work under you, of course. Take them out to the club for drinks or perhaps to a nice restaurant for dinner. Plan the occasional trip with them outstation and see just how rejuvenated they come back to work. After all, that's what the real purpose of work is, isn't it, to have fun with all our hard earned money? Well it's about time you set an example and take your employees out for that very 'fun' yourself! You owe it to them and by so doing, you will harness a bonding with them that is unmatched, one that will go a long way in ensuring that they go out of their way to do their work with pizzazz and not merely for their own monetary benefits or accolades.

Be 'Open' to Change

Oh, you might be telling your employees constantly that 'this is not the way things work around here'. Sure, it might not be the way it has been for the longest time, and perhaps things have really worked out not so bad, after all, with that particular strategy. But you must realize that times are changing. It's no longer the same laid-back world the forefathers of this company lived in. Sometimes, really, we must embrace the facts that things need to change in our workplace!
Believe it or not, but they are the ones who are really 'out' there and might sometimes have an understanding of the market that we don't. It's really a very fast-paced world we live in today, and things keep on changing all the time. Therefore, if an employee raises his or her hand in that meeting of yours and tells you of an entirely new way in which to go about the task that has been eluding your team for months on end, it might really be a good time to listen to them. And by listening it does not mean hearing what they have to say from one ear and taking it out from another. After all, they might be the managers of tomorrow, you never know. So pay attention to what they have to say. It might be really valuable to the future of your company, after all.

Aspire towards 'Excellence'

There's a reason you've woken up with a spring in your step, and that is because you are driven towards 'excellence' in your work, isn't it? That's why you've reached where you have, after all, to the position of 'manager', because you have been silently in pursuit of excellence all your life. This is exactly what needs to be reflected to your employees. They have to know that you are setting 'high' standards for them; you want them to aspire to do the very best they can. You cannot have it any other way if you expect the results to be just that: 'excellent'. They won't perceive you as someone who merely leaves the 'hard work' to people such as themselves, because it is indeed hard work that goes a long way in making sure that you can indeed reach the pinnacle of success and take your work to higher standards. So, in whatever tasks you have allocated for yourself, make sure you aspire to accomplish them with an unparalleled finesse and watch how your employees begin to emulate you in the near future!

Today the customer has so many choices. No matter what industry you are in or what product it is you are trying to sell, the important thing to remember is that the end customer always has a 'choice', and it is that little bit of difference in the end which comes about in your striving towards perfection, that really makes all the difference in the decision that your customer finally makes. Make sure you set only the highest standards for your employees, but at the same time do not allow those standards to be 'daunting' or perhaps even 'impossible'. You might figure that if your sales team achieves even seventy percent of the 'mammoth' target you have set them then your work will be done. But the truth is, people are not satisfied with seventy percent. They want to impress you by making sure that sales target is achieved a one hundred percent. And if they find that it is simply out of their reach, then they might really get most demoralized in the process, which will only serve to hinder their performance. So get realistic and set those targets high and make sure you motivate your employees hard enough to achieve those targets. There is of course no substitute to 'perfection'. Make sure your employees approach their work with the same mindset as well.

Manage your Time

True, we all know that 'time management' is in essence the art of getting all our jobs done, professional or personal, in a given span of time without being heckled and frustrated. Of course it is vital that we make our employees realize the value of time and delegate work to them that comes with certain deadlines, but it is most critical to 'prioritize' the work that we dish out to them.

What this means is that, if there is something of top priority that needs to be done, you might want to set your employee working on that first thing in the morning, when he or she is fresh and high on their levels of concentration.

What is really important here is that you might not want to rush them into finishing the most crucial jobs: after all, there's a reason they have been shortlisted by you as being 'crucial', after all. You don't wish to rush your employees into them, leading to a shoddy outcome in the process. You might wish to accord them a little more time on important projects, because they can make up the time later on by finishing the 'smaller', lesser important tasks in a jiffy towards the end of the day or perhaps even week. So it is critical to 'prioritize' the work you give your employees.

The same goes for you, as well. Make sure that you delegate the work on hand ion the most efficient fashion, freeing yourself for the tasks that 'you' are best equipped to handle. You will notice that you have more and more time to do other tasks that you might not have been able to take on if your management skills were weak and you ended up making a mess of the way you managed your time.

Stare that 'Conflict' in the Face

Whether it's at home or at work, there are problems that are bound to crop up. At work, for instance, there are several issues that can arise that can be very 'emotionally charged' and if you don't deal with these in a delicate manner, things might just flare up and get out of hand, leading to fights within the office, causing unnecessary tension that hinders the productivity of your team, and perhaps even the possibility of an employee resigning in frustration. These can be because of things like 'compensation', 'cost-cutting' or perhaps even 'layoffs'. A lot of times we tend to avoid these alarmingly huge issues, postponing them for later because we simply don't have the confidence to deal with them in the given moment.

Learn the Art of 'Motivation'

Everyone in this world needs to be motivated, even you. You can't wake up in the morning dreading the day of work ahead of you. That simply won't allow you to get your work done efficiently. There's a reason that a lot of people out there quit their jobs from time to time, and that is because they are simply not 'motivated' enough in their 'current' jobs.

So, if you thought that motivation was all about 'money', think again. There are a lot of other things that motivate people, such as spending time with their family. Make sure that you grant your employee that leave he's been planning to take his family to the 'backwaters' for so many years. After all, it will only be for a few days but your employee will most certainly come back charged, refreshed and rejuvenated. After all, there's a reason that we all work, and even though money might be the primary reason, it's really indirectly so that we can live our lives with greater happiness from the luxuries that come with it. And if your employee cannot take

116

his family for that 'holiday' they have been pining for so long, then they might perhaps wonder why on earth they are even working, after all. It gives a wrong signal. After all, they are not your slaves.

Take Responsibility for your Mistakes

We have already seen how saying 'sorry' when we have done something wrong can really go a long way in changing the way your employees think of you. But what if 'they' make a mistake? Do you unnecessarily fire them whenever they do? Unless the mistake is gargantuan and one that is really not expected of them, you might want to take responsibility for them. Yes, you heard it correct. After all, you are the leader of the team and therein must take responsibility for the outcome of the team's actions, just like the captain of a football team might take responsibility for his team's loss even though he has scored the opening goal in the match! What this does, really, is frees the people working under you from the 'fear' of making mistakes. Nobody likes a yelling from the boss, but when there is none and the boss has actually gone out of his or her way to take responsibility for 'their' mistake, it makes them see their mistakes in an altogether different light. The good part of this is that they are free to be 'innovative', which might be the very reason that mistake happened in the first place! They will continue to take risks in the future and that can really go a long way in the creation of something that will take your company to greater heights. Because 'thinking outside the box' really does have its benefits, especially when everyone out there has the very same thing to offer.

If you take responsibility for the mistakes of your employees, they will really come to learn from their mistakes. They will feel that they owe it to you to do that, after your ever-gregarious gesture of taking responsibility for the same. On the other hand, if you simply fire them they will more often than not end up feeling undervalued and demoralized. What's more, they will be so scared of ever

117

making a mistake again that they will not go out of their way to be 'creative' as far as their work is concerned, working within the mundane framework of the objectives that have been assigned to them, not having the confidence to do something innovative that can really help your company, simply because you were all too harsh with them when they made that single mistake. In the end, it 'is' you, really, that is responsible for the results of your team, and how you react when your employee makes a mistake is really critical in how their long-term results might turn out to be. Everyone makes mistakes, after all. Make sure that your employees only grow through the process of making mistakes.

Never stop Learning

Okay, so you know the recipe for success for most of the people who have made it big out there in the corporate world? It's the fact that they are willing to 'learn' all the time. The very fact that you are reading this book means that you are willing to embrace all the different 'techniques' out there to become a better manager. But you have to understand that it doesn't stop here. True, the techniques enlisted herein will help make you a superfluous manager, but you must understand that there is always scope for improvement, no matter how good you are. And so o matter how much you learn, now and in the course of time to come, there will always be plenty of new material out there that might make you glean something not included in this e book because there is nothing such as too much knowledge. It is knowledge that makes us grow, as human beings and helps hone our skills at the workplace. You could even sign up for some e learning courses on the net: anything to sharpen your management skills more and more.

The idea here is to 'learn and practice', over and over again, and we will find ourselves going a long way to become that great manager we always wanted to be, 'tricking' our employees really into believing we are really the best, because, no matter how well intentioned we are and 'in spirit' with the values we expound, the 'message' has to go through, really, to our intended audience, our employees, of course, and the only way to do that is by using the techniques enlisted here and in various other books and sources, which really work in a 'hypnotic' fashion towards making our employees reach the peak of their performance!

Stick to that 'decision'

Not being sure about even one decision will have the effect of making your employees think that you are really unsure about everything you do or say. They will be less likely to take you seriously in the future, and this will affect their levels of productivity at work. If you really want to seat an example to your employees about the kind of confidence that you have, you must really stick to your decisions once you have made them. Sometimes it can be refreshing to see that things really do work out in the end when you stick to a particular train of thought even though several doubts might have disparaged you from continuing to stick to the very same decision. Also, don't waste too much time when you have to make a decision.

You might think that by spending a lot of time deliberating you might really be making it simpler for yourself to really stick to that decision, after all, but the truth is, the best decisions are really made on impulse or in a short period of time.

Wasting too much time obsessing over the decision you are going to make only makes you look 'unsure' in the minds of your employees, even though the decision you might have finally arrived at is one that you feel is 'solid'. Even though you might not change that decision later, you have already made a mistake by sending out the wrong signal to your employees, making them feel that you are really not so sure about the decision you have made and, ironically, other things as well.

Manage that 'Money'

Of course, the key of every successful enterprise is to make lots of money, and more and more of it in the time to come, of course. You have learned to manage time well, but you have to learn the very important lesson that if you don't know how to manage your company's money, then the time management will have practically no purpose at all. You might not want to splurge on that company vacation for your team if your company is making losses. After all, the very fact that makes a company successful is the fact that more money comes 'in' rather than 'going out'.

You have to assess the amount of expenditure you need to incur at all times, making sure that the economics of your company are not compromised. After all, it is the company that pays the salary of all your employees, and if it is going downhill, then you might be faced very soon with the very real possibility of 'downsizing', all because you and others in your organization were not all that careful with the money that flowed into its coffers.

You can learn about money management by reading some books on the same. Perhaps you might feel like you are learning arithmetic again, and this might not be particularly pleasing to you especially if 'Math' was not your favorite subject at high school, but these are the drills you really have to go through. Being a manager means that you are responsible enough to handle your company's money well, and there will be several times when you will be faced with the situation of doing the same. Some might find themselves managing money more than others. No matter what capacity you have in managing money in your organization, make sure you do a pretty good job at it!

Personal Improvement

Of course you are open to the idea of learning things, which is the very reason you are reading this e book in the very first place. But there are certain 'personal' issues you have that might 'cloud' your vision even after you have read this book, and these are the very issues that only one person is capable of identifying and weeding out effectively: you yourself! Perhaps you have a problem with controlling your temper.

You have already read in this book how you should never take out your personal problems on your staff. But you have not learned how to manage your 'temper' which might really be something that has assumed chronic proportions, and something that can be best dealt with by going to a professional who is adept with dealing with these issues.

You have to understand that if you don't take care of your own problems, then it will impact everyone around you. Perhaps you are not all that effective as a communicator. You've reached where you are through sheer hard work and determination but your communication skills are simply not up to the mark. What do you do then? Do you take a course on communicating better? Why you most certainly do!

Take the 'much needed' Break

Sometimes you're really a 'jerk' at work because you're simply too 'stressed', even when things might be going great for you at work. These are the times when you might want to introspect a little and try to find out exactly what it is that's 'getting to you'. More often than not you will come to the realization that you have been working too hard and the thing that you need most of all is a 'vacation'.

You might be thinking, 'No way! Vacation: and me? When there are so many things I have to do? We'll have you even considered the fact that there might really be 'so many things' to do because your efficiency has gone down the drain because you have been working too hard and for too long? Think about it. Exactly how are you at work these days? Do you come smiling into your office every morning or do you arrive grumpy, cursing the janitor under your breath simply because there was a piece of paper in the hallway that he forgot to have picked up?

Celebrate the Little 'Successes'

Of course, the big picture is what you all are aiming for.

Everyone knows that, most of all you. But when certain 'milestones' are achieved along the way to attaining that 'big picture', you might wish to celebrate those too. Plan a surprise dinner party for your employees in the night. They deserve it, for working hard to reach that milestone. That will serve as an incentive to make them work all the harder to reach that next milestone, and that is extremely important, because that is what the 'big picture' is all about, isn't it, the amalgamation of several little milestones along the way? Celebrating the small successes will go a long way in making your employees feel that they are appreciated all that much more by you, and that you are really going out of your way to be nice to them. What's more, it solidly fixes you as a very 'real' part of the team, rather than being some evil boss in a 'James Bond' movie that the employees cannot see but only hear. It makes you 'one of them'.

Go for 'Opportunity' versus 'Capacity'

You must understand that it is not really the 'size' of your team that matters, it is the quality of the work that is done by them that really does, in the end. For this treason you might wish to not hire too many people and instead hire less people who you pay more.

This of course is most beneficial because when you pay people a good sum of money as salary, then they of course work much better for you than they would if their salaries were just a pittance. What's more, you're really paying for 'quality', so when you hire more experienced and capable people, you will get far more work done in the end than if you had a team of under-skilled people working for you at the same total cost of the 'fewer' employees who were far more skilled and experienced.

So it's not really a matter of paying 'less' in totality. You are paying the very same sum of money in 'totality' but at the same time extracting far more output in the process by having a core of fewer, highly skilled workers. You might even consider laying off some people if the need arises, because no matter how harsh it might seem, in the end it really 'is' business after all, and that means that if there is no choice other than to sack a few employees, then there really isn't.

See the 'Human' in Others

A lot of people haven't really done as well in high school as you have, perhaps. But that doesn't mean they might not be capable of doing well in the workplace, contrary to all the ideas we grew up with. Some of them might even stutter in that all too important interview with you, but that should not be a reason you dismiss them as candidates for the job. You must realize that it is good 'human beings' that make the best employees, and you could start by looking for that first in the interview. It's really more of an intuitive process but never underestimate the power of intuition when it comes to selecting a person for the job in mind.

Don't be bitten by the 'Jealous' Bug

It might seem as a bit of a rude shock to you, that the employee working under you is really making more money

123

than you are! Of course it will, you reckon. I mean, you're their manager. This is essence means that you really should be making a lot more money than them. Wrong!

Your employee might earn more money than you, on account of the various commissions they accrue, and it is very easy, really, to get 'jealous' of them and possibly even angry with them, simply because they are making more money than you, their 'manager', and that is something that is most clearly unacceptable. Of course, given a choice you would not witch positions with them, because that would mean that you would have to drop the 'manager' tag, but the fact is that it is really alright for them to be earning that kind of money, simply because they are merely 'doing their job' and are most entitled to it. The best thing, you feel, would be to find a way to 'cut' their rates of commission, but that would only serve to demoralize them and ensure that your targets were not completed with the efficacy that they hitherto were. People feel rewarded and appreciated by money, and it's really a good thing for you as well, because it means that the targets that you have set out for them are being achieved and that means you can sleep better at night, right?

You still don't think so, because you feel that it's really 'not right' for your employee to earn more money than you, but there is nothing out there that states something like that in legal terms, and if you can't deal with then, well then you just have to try all the harder to realize that everyone is entitled to their own share of happiness in this world, and just because you are a 'manager' does not mean that you are entitled to more. Think about it. You have the position you have coveted for so long, that of a manager. Let them have more money than you. After all, the cornerstone for success for you is having a 'happy team', and if that extra money is making them happy, then so be it!

Chapter 18

The 'Right' Amount of Work

You know what they say, about an idle mind being the devil's workshop. If you give them too less work then they will really find themselves being demotivated, even though they are constantly meeting their targets and keeping you happy.

Of course, there really isn't such a thing as 'enough' when it comes to achieving things for your company, and if you find that the targets you have set your employees are not high enough, you might wish to set them a tad bit higher, while at the same time making sure they don't go over the roof, of course!

Don't chase that Promotion Blindly

Since you've gotten to manger status, after all, you might have been bitten by the 'promotion' bug and seek to climb another rung of the ladder. Of course you want more. It's basic human nature, for crying out loud. But you must understand that by constantly rubbing shoulders with upper management and spending time on tasks that are not related to the projects you have at hand, you might actually cause those very 'critical' projects to fall through the cracks, simply because you did not show the level of involvement in them that your employees have. This will only cause your employees to think of you as nothing but an egotistical 'jerk', who does not care about them simply because he is not being a part of the 'team' where it comes to the project at hand. Think about the captain of a football team. He will work as hard, perhaps even harder than his teammates, to ensure that they win the match in progress. Well then why shouldn't you? Make sure that you are there in the place that counts in the first place, more involved with the cause of your employees rather than seeking ways to further your own cause. Besides, if you end up being lackadaisical about your work, it might not really be such a good idea after all, because getting promoted relies heavily on your achievements, and in your attempt to get to the top, you might really be killing the 'goose' that will help you get there, the completion of the work you have at hand, that is. So make sure you do whatever it takes to get promoted, because we all deserve to go up in life, there's nothing wrong with that; but make sure you stay as a team player as well, because that's where your responsibility truly lies. Make sure you have that priority in check and you might be getting one step closer to that promotion you have been seeking for a very long time, after all!

Appreciate the 'Individual'

Everyone in this world is different, as are you. This means that everyone has a working style that is all their own. Now, the easiest way to be conceived of as a jerk by your employees is by telling them that you don't particularly like 'their' working style, and that you would rather they did it 'your' way. Think about it: what is the ultimate objective here? Well, you want to get the work done, don't you? Then why on earth should the way the employee goes about reaching the goal, bother you at all? Perhaps he might really be doing things in a more efficient manner. You cannot know until you let him or her go through with the way they do it, to completion. You have to give them a chance to express their own individuality, or they are really going to think of you as a 'jerk', after all.
Network
One word, it's as simple as that. You have to make sure you take your team members for seminars and conferences; places they can meet other people and share valuable ideas.

That removes the sense of them working in isolation. As we all know, man is not a solitary animal and by exposing them to a large host of events and people, you will be reinforcing in them the thought that you do indeed care for them by going out of your way to broaden their horizons. Besides, networking is a great way of broadening the visibility of your organization; getting it out there, having it noticed. You can never expect success if you constantly live within your shell, so make sure you get that 'turtle head' out and keep exploring! You will find that not only will it provide a refreshing environment for your employees who will be highly indebted to you for the same, and you will also increase their levels of productivity as well. Nothing better than having happier and more productive employees, is there?

Look for a Mentor

As the manager of your team you are nothing short of being their 'mentor'. And as such, there is no possible way to be one's mentor than to have a mentor yourself: to experience in firsthand the positive presence of a mentor in your life is the easiest way to inculcate those very same values which you can then pass on to your team members! Look for people you might know, people who are highly successful and happy in their jobs, people with a greater level of experience than you. Ask them if they would be kind enough to be your mentor. You could come to them from time to time with any problems that you might and they will happily guide you through them with ease, because they too will feel privileged that you have chosen them as your mentor, after all!

When you have a mentor you will really pick up those subconscious cues from them in the process of them guiding you through the course of your work, and believe it or not, it will reflect in the way you handle your own employees at work! Because no matter what you think of yourself, you are not perfect: come to think of it, not even your mentor is. But he or she is definitely in a good position to guide you in the process of management.

So find that role model in your life, someone you wish to emulate. You will be amazed at the things you learn for them. After all, like we have discussed earlier, there is never a dearth of knowledge out there as far as it comes to management skills, and what better way to learn than by having a living human example who is highly successful at what he or she does?

Taking time to breathe correctly

There is a very good reason why people take up meditation. It enables them to balance the influences that come into their minds and learn to breathe in a certain way that encourages the right amount of oxygen to be circulating in the bloodstream. If you work on overload all of the time, maybe devoting 20 minutes of your day to meditation would be the most productive thing that you can do because the clarity that you get from meditation makes it a worthwhile exercise.

If you are worried about packing enough hours into the day, set your alarm an hour earlier and do your meditation before breakfast. This helps you to greet the day with a balanced mind and a calm approach. You may not be aware of it but most people only use the top part of the lungs when they breathe. This means that oxygen flow is affected and it also means that panic can set in. Meditation puts this right by teaching you a method of deep breathing that encourages your sympathetic nervous system to carry out all of its functions in your body. A more efficient body means a more efficient mind.

To meditate, you simply sit in a hard chair and keep your back straight. Your feet should be flat on the floor. Your hands are placed one on top of the other – palms upward and thumbs touching. Breathe in through the nostrils to the count of 8, hold the breath to the count of 4 and breathe out to the count of 10. You repeat this process over and over again and at the same time, you try to keep thoughts from entering your head. When they do, you simply observe them as if they were not part of your life and then let them go. Do not attach any emotions to these thoughts because they are not given credence until you do. Learning to let go is one of the best disciplines that you can encompass into your life because it serves you very well in the workplace too. It also makes you a better listener and you may pick up some very valuable ideas along the way.

Meditation is also an absolute necessity for today's warrior, and in developing mental toughness. This really is among one of the most effective instruments for changing your state of mind, and also thus providing you with the endurance, hardiness and feel of how serene you have become, you want to pick the best way to answer your feelings and emotions.

Meditation is just the custom of focusing the brain, of draining the mind of random thoughts and anxiety that cripple our discipline in life, and also of course learning in order to steer clear of diverting thoughts and impulses. It happens fast and creates a fantastic mental field and at this way, it's the ideal for quieting the mind. This is truly the way to be at peace with yourself.

Moreover, is the fact that meditation educates one to divert from the fears, your own instincts as well as your own desires. Conscious meditation educates one to allow your mind to float by with no bothering of you personally, whilst transcendentally calms the mind.

This really is actually a huge means to be relaxed, changing your physiology, once anxious or excited; you are now in control of your ideas and activities. People that meditate are both wealthier and not as readily riled, and that frees them to do something from the absolute most and be efficient at everything they do.

In the end, meditation can be just a huge means to recharge your batteries also gain extra electricity, which then gives you the ability to accomplish your aims.

When you meditate, you allow your subconscious mind to rest and this makes it sharper when it needs to be, later on in the workplace. Meditation has many other benefits such as lowering the blood pressure, reducing the speed of the heartbeat and allowing you to approach the day in a positive frame of mind. The practice needs to be incorporated into your life as a matter of course, each and every day because the more you do it, the better you become at doing it and it really will change your views in life to such an extent that you will feel able to conquer all of the workload that you have.

Drinking water

I am never sure why so many people leave this very important ingredient out of their lives. You need to drink about 8 glasses of water a day and if you start the day right and begin early, you will find that you keep your body hydrated and that you tend to feel healthier when you do this. Many people who suffer from stress do so because the body is trying to tell them that it needs water. This isn't just when you are hot. It isn't just when you are thirsty. Keeping the body able to move and feel good without the onset of inflammation also helps to keep your brain sharp and ready to take on the tasks of the day.

Understand your 'Own' Boss

Yes, like we have discussed, you too have a boss of your own. It's not like you are in absolute control of things simply because you have reached the managerial position. You have to know that there are things that your own boss will expect from you, the directions in which he or she might wish you to proceed. If you don't spend enough time with your boss trying to get a clear understanding of what he or she wants, then it really might not work out all too well for you in the end, because it might well serve as an impediment in the future, when you are looking to get things done and your boss has to intervene and discard the valuable work done by you and your employees simply because your communication with him or her was not clear right from the very beginning. This can be thoroughly demoralizing for your employees when all their work goes wasted merely because the channels of communication between you and your boss were not clear. So make sure you understand your 'boss', before you get down to making those action plans for your employees!

Learn to 'Divide'

So, you have a team of people working for you. Have you ever thought of dividing them into smaller teams? We have already discussed how you can have 'leaders' of specific teams, thereby motivating those same key employees to perform better, but we haven't gone into just how important it is to 'divide' the people working towards your goals into several 'teams'. Let's look at why this is so crucial.
You have to understand that people work better together in 'smaller' groups. The reason for this is really quite simple. There is a better communication involved when people interact with each other within smaller groups; it really makes it a lot easier to get things done in this way. Let's say for example you have around fifty clients. You could then divide your team members who total twenty into five groups of four each, each group being assigned to ten clients. This makes it a lot easier as the focus is divided equally amongst

your employees, who will do a much better job rather than if they were to be working all together in that initial single group of twenty! Each team will take responsibility for their own set of clients and that really makes things a whole lot simpler.

Show that 'Passion'

So, you might be an excellent strategist in the boardroom, but if the employees don't see that 'enthusiasm' in your body language, how on earth will you expect them to get fired up sufficiently to work for you with pizazz?
You have to be most animated when discussing the goals your company is striving for; you have to look like you really want them much more than they do, setting a benchmark for them, pushing them to your level of passion. If you yourself look unmotivated whilst you drawl out your objectives for the company, then you will get just that in return from them: a lackluster approach towards the goals you have just stenciled out for them. You have to show them that you are manically inspired to achieve those goals. You have to drive them sufficiently to reach the same.
In the end, you must realize that in effect you really 'are' the role model for your employees, and they will thereby pick up little cues from you every step of the way. If you show them a greater deal of confidence and gusto in the boardroom, the chances that they will imbibe just that from you are manifold. So go out there and show them the hunger in your eyes, the level of dedication that you yourself have towards achieving those goals you have just set down on paper, and watch them go out there with that same steely resolve in their eyes, ready to take on your clients with an ever increased sense of gusto!

Don't be Scared of Hiring the 'Best'

Yes, when you're in the process of hiring employees for your team, you might indeed find that some of them are better or perhaps even more qualified than you. All they lack is the experience, and if you don't give it to them in the fear that they might take your job someday, you might really be making the biggest mistake of your life.

The truth is, you need the 'best' people in your team: that's what's going to make all the difference in the end. And there's nothing better than when you employ someone who is really inherently much better than you. That will only serve to increase the drive and efficacy within your own team and keep your employees inspired. You need a good person; that's what organizations are really all about. So make sure you get the very best, even if that means they might really be much better than you!

Have a positive attitude.

When you have a positive attitude, you will look at all situations as positive. Even the negative ones, you'll see some positivity in them and take the situation to your advantage. This helps you to address the issue on board in a positive way and thus, positive results will be witnessed. Do not look at life situations in a negative way. Instead, take them as stepping stones to lead you towards your success.

Set your goals.

Setting your goals is the first step that gives you a direction as they give you a predetermined destiny of where you want to reach. It's much wise to set goals that are achievable and realistic, so that they won't make you give up when you are just half-way. At the same time, your goals should have a time limit set. Set goals with reasonable time limit for example monthly, quarterly, half-year, full year or other short-term goals. Long-term goals may be set up to five years and above. When you have your goals set, you will be able to direct your energy, time and resources towards achieving those goals. Goals give you a mission.

Make a plan for your activities.

Your plan will include the activities you wish to do that are directed by your goals. Dedicate enough time to every single task and ensure you finish it within the allocated time. If you strictly follow your plan, you will always be finishing your activities in time. This will help you to achieve your set goals within the time set and thus, you are most likely to succeed in your mission and life.
Do one task at a time.
Mixing many tasks at a time will lead to ineffectiveness in all the tasks involved. This will waste a lot of your precious time that you would be using to accomplish your mission, which is to achieve your goals. Concentrate on doing one task at a time and be sure to do it as perfectly as you can. Then do the next task on your to-do list. This will help you minimize time wastage and therefore, you will witness more productivity and success in due course.

Always be highly motivated.

Being motivated means your interest is stimulated towards a given direction. Self-motivation assists you to do everything you have to in order to achieve your success. It helps you do the tasks you have identified in the plan in a happier way and with no wastage of time. Be motivated towards achieving your set goals and never give up in whatever you do.

Develop a positive stress for your future goals.
This will always keep your mind and concentration directed towards achieving your set goals. It will make you gather all relevant information, resources and ideas related to your goals. In addition, it will help you ensure proper time

management with less or no wastage. With the ideas, materials & information you have gathered, plus proper time management, you will end up stepping closer to your goals and success.

Take risks.

Always be prepared to take risks in activities and ideas that can positively affect your life. Never let fear of risk overtake you, rather, take the risk and you might find yourself up the ladder. Fearing risks will make you fear implementing any idea and therefore, fewer opportunities for success. Take risks, even if you fail, you will have learnt one way not to do it again. So you will try other methods different from the one that failed. And it is not always that you will fail on something, especially if the probability of positive results is high.

Read many books.

There are many books, magazines and novels out there that contain stories of successful people in the world. Reading these resources will inspire and motivate you towards achieving your dream. At the same time, you can borrow some ideas or techniques that you can apply in life and end up increasing and improving your performance. This will eventually lead you to success in life.

Ensure regular exercise.

Regular body exercise helps your body cells to be active. Even a simple 10-15 minutes exercise adds a lot in life as it helps you relax your mind and body. With a fresh mind and body, you will be active in your activities and your productivity & effectiveness will be high. At the same time, you will be able to make right decisions with your fresh mind and this can lead you to succeed in your life goals. You can do some simple press-ups, jogging, or even football.

Have Self-belief.

Always believe in yourself. Believe that you have the ability reach your goals and never lose hope. Believe that you will make it and for sure, you will. As long as you believe in yourself and in achievement of your goals, you will input all your effort towards achieving them. Add your expertise in doing your tasks and this will help you to produce more and more leading you to success.
Be open-minded and up-to-date.
Let your mind be open to new information and ideas as you ensure you are updated with the current trends in your field of concern. If there is a new product in the market of your interest, be the first to know and take it as an opportunity. You create a new product similar to the one you saw, or if you are a businessperson, you can get some for your shop and avail them to your customers. In case of new methods of work, you will be among the firsts to know and can implement if found it good. This can lead you to success. Otherwise, you will be outdated in the market and make fewer sales and hence, failure and losses will be your results.

Celebrate your success.

When you have succeeded in one goal, it is wise to set some time apart and celebrate whether alone or with some friends or family. After all, why are you working so hard to succeed? It's because you want to enjoy life in the future and future starts from next minute. You see even in employments when some goals are achieved, there is a small celebration with the employees to appreciate and motivate them. Appreciating yourself keeps you motivated to proceed to the next goals.

Put your Creator first.

In all you do, remember to give thanks to your creator (God) for all He has done for you. Pray Him to help you and guide your thinking & activities towards achieving the goals you have set. Try to do good always so that the Most High can hear and answer your prayers. With Him leading you, you will definitely end up achieving your goals and succeeding in this life.

Assign Projects in 'Slices'

So, you have your team ready to work on that all too important project they just can't wait to get their hands on. But have you ever wondered if it might really be best if you give it to them in little doses rather than in one single shot? Of course your team knows the 'big picture' as far as this single task is concerned. But when it comes to the process of them undertaking it, they might really come to realize that they feel overpowered because the task really seems to be quite daunting, after all, a far cry from what they had imagined it would work out to be. It is for this reason solely that you might wish to give them that project in 'slices'.

After every project is completed, it's like a milestone, isn't it, one that you will perhaps celebrate, like we have suggested doing earlier in this book? Well then you might wish to consider the little 'slices' you break every individual project into, as several 'mini' milestones along the way. So every time your team members reach every mini milestone out there, you could give them a pat on the back and egg them to move forward onto the next one. This will do wonders for their confidence and make them feel appreciated, of course. There's simply no better way to get that project done than in this way; it keeps your employees going and prevents them from being burned out when it comes to doing their work!

Chilly Showers

Chilly showers raise your metabolism, so they also assist you to produce a lot more testosterone plus additionally they also cause a flooding or adrenaline. They are able to in fact strengthen your defense mechanisms also. To put it differently, they truly are actually great for you personally and also a good means to begin every own day.
But in an identical period they harm and they all also suck. This really is an awful jolt for the machine also it's really the previous thing that you wish to do.
That is just the reason it's the best for the warrior practice. Maintaining chilly showers takes exceptional mental area of course in the event that you may force yourself to complete so daily, then you definitely may reach virtually any such thing.

So, that since it's an enjoyable activity, even 007 action start Daniel Craig reported that he would take cold showers daily, and especially when doing James Bond. Currently there exists a warrior which you might manage to become like!

Be Grateful

Have you ever considered the fact that you might really not be smiling all that much at work, being so clearly bogged down by the work you have at hand? Don't you know just how detrimental this can be to the overall atmosphere in that boardroom where you conduct your meetings with your employees?
You have to understand that your employees are first of all human beings and they deserve to be treated with compassion and love. When you smile, you are doing just

138

that. It doesn't take all that much, really, and when you smile at them first thing in the morning then it pretty much sets the tone for the rest of the day to come. What's more, smiling will make 'you' feel a lot better the very moment you do it. That's yet another reason to smile. You could even add something to that smile of yours, like perhaps a compliment to an employee of yours, remarking on how sharply they are dressed today and just how spiffy they look. You could also simply thank them for being there. After all, they are special because they are a part of 'your' team, and therefore have a significant value in your life as compared to mere strangers on the street!

Finding Time

Where does all the time go? Is it under the cushion, hiding behind the sofa, or did it sneak out the door when your back was turned? Who knows, but it just seems to disappear when you need it most. Most inconvenient. But if you want to achieve more in your life, then you are going to have to track the pesky thing down and make it work for you instead of against you. Here's how. We all lead busy lives, and when we have finally finished the day's work, fed the kids, walked the dog, done the after-school activities, phoned mum and sorted out the car insurance, all you can manage is to make yourself a drink and sit back in the sofa for a few minutes before it's time for bed.

When you add it all up, we spend a lot of time watching other people live their lives (or made-up people living their made-up lives) rather than living our own. It's important to relax: we all need downtime and some quiet time before going to bed will help us get a good night's sleep, but there are other options than reality TV, YouTube, Facebook and Netflix.

Relaxing by doing an activity you enjoy can be just as effective and a lot more rewarding. Whether it's something creative like knitting, painting or crafting, or playing an instrument, doing some creative writing, or some other hobby or pastime, there are many alternatives that can help you relax and give your mind and body a chance to unwind.

These less passive forms of relaxation can be just as effective and have the added benefits of giving you great pleasure and the satisfaction of seeing a positive result at the end. And you're less likely to be tempted to snack and have that extra glass of wine, so your body wins too.
Cutting back on screen time can release a huge amount of time to help you achieve more.

It's important that you do still have time to switch off and truly relax. That could be watching a great movie, reading a good book, catching with your friends or spending time with your loved ones. Watching crappy TV, reading trashy novels or scrolling through social media can be good too, but is very addictive and before you know it the whole evening has gone. Watching other people live their lives on TV or Facebook doesn't help you relax and it builds up a false picture of how exciting everyone else's lives are, because you don't see the everyday routine tasks that occupy most of our waking hours.

Eat Well

Most of us aren't fueling our bodies as well as we should. In fact, we shovel so much rubbish down our throats that it's a miracle that we can function at all. If we had the same approach to fueling our cars they wouldn't get off the garage forecourt.
We all know that we're supposed to eat more fruit and vegetables, to cut down on the sweets and the fatty foods, but

it seems so hard and the snacks, ready meals and takeaways are so convenient and so tasty.

You don't have to wait until your body starts to break before making a change. And you don't have to change everything at once. In fact, unless you have an urgent medical need, making small changes is probably best, as it's easier to stick with the change and you can monitor the results more effectively.

Sleep More

If you spend all of your waking hours worried about your workload, then you won't achieve very much. It's far better to make sure that you get your eight hours of sleep. The release of hormones into the body while you sleep helps to mend whatever is not working correctly in your body. It refreshes the mind and helps your concentration levels. Thus, sleep is vital. Put away your computer at a reasonable hour and allow yourself to get a good night's sleep every night if you want to increase your ability to produce.

If you are already achieving things in your life and are looking to achieve even more then it's a fairly safe bet that you probably aren't getting enough sleep. Most of us don't, and those who are most driven probably get less sleep than average.

Here's a quick checklist of signs that could indicate that you aren't getting enough sleep:

You're always grumpy
You're always hungry
You fall asleep as soon as your head hits the pillow
You look tired (kind of gives it away)
You're constantly fighting infections
You're always daydreaming
Little things upset you

141

Even coffee can't fully wake you up
You have no sex drive
You fall asleep watching TV or a film
You're clumsier than normal
Your face is breaking out in spots

If you can check off several of these, there's a good chance that you would benefit from a bit more shut-eye. There's also good evidence linking lack of sleep to excess eating (I know that if I need to work late I have cravings for food, and it's usually not for healthy stuff!), so if you are trying to lose weight, then making sure you are getting enough sleep should help.

We only have 24 hours in a day and if you are trying to get more done then it seems crazy to spend more of the sleeping. But it's not the amount of time you spend doing things, it's how much you get done. Being fully recharged and full of energy means that you are much more productive, more than compensating for the slight reduction in the time available.

There have been studies to show that good programmers are ten times as productive as average programmers, and I'm sure this is similar in other walks of life. It's not because they can write code faster, but because they write the right code, first time. I can imagine it's the same with joiners on a building site: it's not how quickly they can saw the wood; it's about making the right cut first time.
If you are tired from lack of sleep then you're not functioning at your best, and so you are not being as productive as you could be. We're not talking about a slight drop in productivity here, you could easily be less than half as productive or even just 10% as productive as your best. I'm sure you have experienced times when you've come in

to work refreshed and zipped through tasks in minutes that were taking hours' yesterday afternoon.

Don't be tempted to stay up late to finish a project: you'll be much better off going to bed and finishing it in the morning. Not only will it get done in less time, you'll do a better job of it. We make better decisions and fewer mistakes when we are not tired (hence the higher productivity). Everyone around you suffers if you burn the midnight oil: you're just not such good company when you're tired and grumpy.

So to achieve more (and to look better too – it's not called beauty sleep for nothing), go to bed a little earlier tonight.

Exercise

For some, exercise is a dirty word. And in many ways most of our inventions over the years have been designed to reduce the amount of exercise we get in our daily lives. They aren't called labor-saving devices for nothing. But instead of replacing the drudgery of washing clothes by hand with something more fun and exhilarating, like playing with the kids in the park or walking in the countryside, we either spend more time in the office or sitting on the couch watching television. And then we wonder why we suffer from weight gain, heart problems and so on.

Why should you exercise? It will help you live longer. You will feel better. You will have more energy.

Why don't we exercise? It takes time. It's hard work. We might need a shower after. It's too much bother, it's easier just to sit here and keep doing what you're doing.

When you look at it logically, there's no good reason for us not to get at least 30 minutes of good quality exercise a day. It doesn't have to mean putting on Lycra and going to the gym. A brisk walk with the dog is enough to blow the cobwebs away and get your heart working.

Human beings aren't meant to sit around all day: we evolved to be on the move for much of the time. In fact, some believe that the reason humans aren't covered in fur like most mammals is to help us to keep cool when we are active, and that early hunters used to literally run their prey to death. They did this not by being faster, but by keeping going and causing their prey to overheat and collapse from heat exhaustion. This is explained better in the book "Born to Run".

However, simply walking is one of the best forms of exercise. If you can get for a walk in a green space near you then it can also help relax your mind as well as exercise your body. You don't need any special equipment, you don't need to get changed before and after: just grab your jacket and step out the door. It costs nothing yet gives you plenty back.

Grab every chance you can to walk. Walk the dog, walk the kids to school, walk to work, walk to the shops (it's good to support your local shops), walk upstairs instead of taking the lift. The more you do it the better you feel. Use a step counter and see if you can reach 10,000 steps a day.

If you've not been exercising for a while, then walking is probably the best way to start. It's low impact so you are less likely to strain your muscles and joints, yet it helps build muscle tone and improve your circulation. Just by walking each day you can regain your fitness to the point where you can start thinking about other forms of exercise that might have been out of the question before.

Getting out of your seat and walking is one of the best things you can do for your health.

Be Your Own Coach

We can be our own worst critic when we should be our greatest cheerleader. If we make the slightest mistake we beat ourselves up about it instead of congratulating ourselves for how much we got right. I'm not saying we should ignore our errors, but when we talk to ourselves, we should take a leaf from the coach's book.

Most coaches use the sandwich approach when giving feedback: some initial praise, then something to be worked on, and then something positive to finish. You can picture the scene at the poolside as the swimmer reaches the end of the lane, the coach leaning down and saying, "You're swimming well tonight. Watch that left arm entry, but your body position is great." The swimmer gets the information they need to improve their technique but are left feeling good having being praised.

So if you are sitting down after your presentation and you realize that you completely missed one of the key points you wanted to make. You are kicking yourself for messing it up, when you should be focusing on the reactions of the audience. To be brutally honest, most of them will only have heard about fifty percent of what you said anyway. So you missed a bit our, big deal, half of them wouldn't have heard it and the other half probably knew it already. But hey, you just stood up and gave the presentation! Well done you. Sure, it could have been better, but you did it. And next time it will be better.

That's the sort of thing you should be saying to yourself. It helps you build a positive memory of the experience so that next time you will be slightly less nervous and will approach it with more confidence. And the more confident you are, the better you will present. After all, most of the impressions of your audience are from how you came across rather than what you said.

And the best way to build confidence is through praise and positive affirmation.

Perhaps you got up early to write but were distracted by chores and didn't get anything written? You still got up early, that's the first step, tomorrow you can get up early again and those chores are done now so you will be able to write something.

There are many people out there ready to criticize you, to put you down if you should try and stand up and stand out. Don't join them, or you will never succeed. Think of how parents encourage their toddlers to walk: they don't scold them for falling down, they lavish praise when they manage their first few faltering steps into their arms.

We're a bit older now and probably would feel a bit uncomfortable with that level of praise for presenting a paper to the board meeting, but a "good job" from your boss will still make you feel good.

We've all got that inner voice that runs through our head. When you are completely focused on a task it goes quiet, you're in the zone, or flow as developers call it But when you stop and sit back to look over what you've done, that's when your inner voice kicks in big time. You need to take control and first of all find something positive to say to yourself. It doesn't matter what it is, even if it was just to congratulate yourself for working hard for thirty minutes. Now you can find something to be improved, before finishing again with another positive.

This will feel really contrived at first, but stick with it and it will become a habit and will eventually feel natural. Coaches aren't born knowing how to give feedback this way, they were taught it and have practiced it. To begin with it probably felt really awkward for them, but over time it became a habit and it now feels natural and normal to them. And so it will with you if your stick with it and keep finding the positives in what you do.

At first you might struggle to think of something positive, but it doesn't matter how corny it might be, say it anyway. Remember, just doing it is a positive, like all those people finishing hours after the winners at the end of the marathon, they are still way ahead of everyone on the couch. Keep working at it and you will get better at it and you will find more positives to praise. And soon there will be more positives to praise, because you will get better. Well done.

Persistence

I believe the key to achievement is persistence. Talent is an advantage, having a great new idea is fantastic, good connections and access to resources will help, but none of this will take you from where you are now to your goal. It's up to you to get there, one step at a time.
There are so many quotes by that most prolific of authors, Anonymous: "the longest journey begins with a single step", "how do you eat a chocolate elephant? One bite at a time", and of course Aesop's fable of the tortoise and the hare.

So how do you become persistent?

The easiest way is to become persistent is to do something we enjoy doing. Most of us have no problem with being persistent at eating and sleeping. We seem to have no problems fitting this in to our busy schedules every day. If your goal is to achieve something that is your passion and that you love doing, the chances are that you will find to easier to make time for it.

Routine is a great aid to being persistent: we can stumble through our morning ablutions half asleep and manage to wash and brush our teeth without having to exercise our motivational muscles. Making working towards your goal a part of your daily routine will make it much easier to be persistent. Motivation is like a muscle: it gets tired if you use it too much. Adding new activities at the start of the day is easier for most of us because our motivation muscles are still fresh. Get up slightly earlier (not forgetting to go to bed earlier too) and fit in just half an hour of activity and you will be progress steadily and surely towards your goal.

At first it will be hard, and during the first few days and weeks you will have to really flex your motivational muscles, but after a month it will become part of your routine and you won't even have to make a conscious decision to do it.

Thirty minutes is not a lot of time, but repeated every day it soon adds up. And the thing is, that even though you might only be actively doing the activity for a short period, your mind will be working on it at various times throughout the day. You are likely to have ideas and thoughts at various times during the day that you can put to good use the next morning. Or if your goal is more physical in nature, then your mind will work with your muscles to improve your technique as it recalls the activity throughout the day, improving your "muscle memory". You can accelerate this using visualization techniques, boosting the benefits of the training time.

Thirty minutes a day is over 180 hours a year, or four and a half weeks of solid work with no interruptions or distractions. I don't know how many breaks, meetings and other interruptions you have at work, but I would expect that 180 hours would represent at least two months of productive work time. Think about what you could achieve at work in two months: you could make the same progress towards your own goals with just half an hour a day.

There will be frequent threats to time you have planned to dedicate to your activity; if you are travelling or on holiday it can be harder, but you should try and stick to your routine. You might have to move things around a bit, but even doing a little is better than nothing.

Doing a little each day is more likely of success than throwing yourself into your goal, working towards it using every available minute, until you eventually crash and burn.

This tactic can work for a very short period and can be useful when you are trying to get something finished or to meet a deadline, but you will need to schedule a rest and recovery period afterwards and the mental, physical and emotional impacts shouldn't be underestimated.

Making working towards achieving your goal is not only a great strategy for success, the emotional boost from seeing the steady progress is hugely rewarding.

Making Success Routine

Achieving success is supposed to be hard work, a constant struggle against those who don't believe in your dream and are trying to put you down, fighting against the system which is designed to stop people like you from making it. In reality, if often simply comes down to habit. Or more precisely, by adopting the right habits you can form daily routines that will help you achieve success. If you have a look through the self-help section of any bookshop you will see titles like the "seven habits of successful people".

So if it's so easy why aren't we all doing it? Why haven't we all achieved our goals, become millionaires and won Olympic medals? The same reason average waist sizes are increasing: temptation fueled by an increasingly sophisticated marketing industry that is doing its best to keep you buying more of what they are selling and spending your time on what they have to offer.

So take the time to work out what it is that is stopping you from forming successful habits. Find ways to dealing with these barriers or temptations so it is easier for you to do the right things. Then you are giving yourself a good chance to do them often enough for them to become part of your routine and you can form the habits that will help you achieve your goals.

Establish Order

The first step in prioritizing is establishing some kind of order. But lists are ineffective in creating order, since they tend to be both subjective and inflexible. Yet they are what so many people promote to increase productivity.
I bet you've heard this advice before: "Create your 'to-do' list the night before and you'll be certain to progress through every task quickly and efficiently." Was that person a paragon of efficient productivity?
That is a natural consequence of business. Most companies have competing reward systems that prevent efficiency. Of course that's not intentional, but it is inevitable. Sales drives business. Operations function as a check on sales to make sure the win for salespeople makes sense for the organization. The same dynamic exists in small teams within departments.

But these conflicting interests can be overcome; most of the time, with some ease. Consider this: Your team members push to get your time immediately because they know you are busy too, right? Rather than risk their request getting lost, they demand your attention for as long as it takes to clear the item that requires your input off their list. But what if they knew that you had certain blocks of time budgeted for them?

The first way to order your day more effectively is to account for the inevitable interruptions from colleagues. When we build our lists, we try to pack everything possible into the time we spend at the office. I've done it, and so did the people on my teams. We all have a finite amount of time and what feels like an infinite amount of work. With those constraints, we naturally start to feel like every second counts.

Here's how you can quickly and simply solve this problem: Show them that they will have ample opportunity to get items on their list cleared. By giving them a block or, ideally, two blocks of your time every day, your team will learn to bring things to you when you are best able to help them. Many times they will meanwhile find the answer to their problem without even talking with you.

Let your colleagues, coworkers, bosses, employees, and whomever else is on your team know that you are available specifically to offer input on their tasks for whatever they might need from 11:00am to noon, and again from 4:30 to 5:30pm, as an example. That way, if at 9:00am someone on your team realizes they need something from you, they won't panic and try to get it immediately, because they'll know that you've set aside a period of time when you'll be available for them, and it's only a couple hours away.

The second misconception of list-making is the grouping together of similar tasks. This appeals to our sense of logic.

151

Most people believe that, by doing the same or a similar thing over again, they can do it more efficiently. Instead, what happens is that they grow weary of the task; their minds begin to wander and, as they wander, more mistakes are made.

The solution here is almost as simple as it is quickly applied. Structure your day with as few back-to-back tasks of the same type.

Workdays are chaotic. Conflicting requirements send us down a spiral of unproductivity. But when we add order to the mix, we improve our ability to accomplish what we set out in front of us. A list alone is not enough. We need our lists to take into account the needs of those around us, and ourselves. In doing so, we work smarter.

Chapter 19

What to "Do", What to "Delegate", and What to "Defer"

Have you ever worked with an individual who needed to do everything? That level of immersion in everything is common in our workplaces. We all know someone who acts that way. Many of us can acknowledge that we have done the same thing ourselves.

When we stop to consider the relative importance of what we need to accomplish, we can usually sort out which things we must do ourselves. Our problem is that we approach our work all too often with a sense of desperation. That holds true especially when we are racing to finish deadlines. Ironically, this moment is when we most need to delegate and, thanks to the pressure we feel, when we are least capable of delegating.

Economists refer to this concept as economy of scale. Whenever you delegate a task to someone with greater expertise in that particular task, you maximize productivity. Prioritizing the best division of labor ensures that you can focus on work you will do quickly and efficiently. The other part of the trap of delegation is accepting that something can be deferred.

Why and How to Disconnect and Unplug
Stop everything you're doing. Your phone wants your attention. The two-tone chime signals you and interrupts your train of thought. Sometimes it's an important message... but sometimes it's "lol" with a smiley face.

Distinguishing between the important messages that we need to receive and the less important ones takes up a chunk of our time. These and other distractions destroy our productivity. In those moments we spend evaluating the message to decide how necessary it was to respond, we lose our train of thought. That's why the next lesson of prioritization is disconnecting from distractions.

Multi-tasking is a form of "productive" distraction. Employers desire it because being a capable multi-tasker suggests you can do more than one thing at one time. The problem with multi-tasking is that it never works out the way it is supposed to.

Distractions come in many forms. Try it yourself and see how much of a difference it makes. Spend one afternoon this week with your phone off, your email down, and your phone on DND.

Unplugging from distractions helps pave the way for its antithesis; when you don't have people and things jarring you from your work, you can focus your energy fully on completing tasks.

Chapter 20

Maintain your Focus

With your devices now silent and your environment calm, all you must do now is focus on the work to be done. If you have established a sense of order and delegated and deferred tasks, your "to-do" list should be fairly short. But it may not be short enough.

A list of more than three or four items has built-in distractions. So pare down the list to the bare minimum. Here's where you can ruthlessly apply the second rule of delegating and deferring. Now that you have your true core tasks, set a timer for 90 to 100 minutes. You will use that time to focus on a single item on your list, until the timer goes off or the task is completed.

After you complete the tasks or when the timer goes off, stop and take a mandatory twenty-minute break. Go for a quick walk around the parking lot. Pull out a book you have been reading and go through a short chapter. Do something that is completely disconnected from your job. Then, once you have taken your break, plug your PC back into the network, turn your phone back on, and see to the messages you have received while you were focusing.

When you first try this, you will either grossly underestimate the time you need or you will wildly overestimate the time these tasks take. That's okay. This is all part of a learning curve that eventually leads to you becoming an expert at prioritizing your day and maximizing your productivity.

Not exactly. In fact, the first thing to do is to review the component tasks of each step. These reports require data to be compiled, formatted, and then printed out. The three-item list is now five. Thankfully, data compilation can be delegated to a business analyst and the distribution can be handled by an intern. With the list back at three, our colleague can await receipt of the data before formatting and reviewing the reports. Then they can be printed out.

How long this will take is a matter of trial and error to start. The first time this employee undertook the task, it took far longer than the time that had been budgeted. The second run through took a little less than what had been allotted. By the third time, the employee set the time for the exact amount needed to complete the work.

As we develop better productivity habits, we train ourselves to be more mindful, not only of deadlines, but how long things take. That is the kind of benefit that we gain from a proper focus on the tasks we have prioritized.
You can probably list at least five things that will distract you at moment's notice. If you can't, take a look at what's going on around you. Is the television on your favorite show when you're planning on doing housework? Or does your browser magically divert to social media when you're trying to accomplish a project for work? These items are a couple of the biggest distractions that I have found by just looking around and noticing. Whatever your distractions are, try to stay focused on what you're doing at that moment in time. The distraction will always be there later.

Remind Yourself of What You're Doing

Some people get distracted very easily. So, by constantly reminding yourself of what your task is and what you hope to accomplish, you can reroute your attention to the correct task. Distractions have a funny way of having us do things that we shouldn't be doing when we're trying to accomplish something!

Block Websites that Distract You

The great part is, others have recognized this and created ways to keep yourself in check while you're on the computer. If it's a certain website that distracts you, block it until you're done. There are also programs that you can purchase and install on your computer in order to achieve the same outcome. Find a way to get away from the websites that distract you!

Learn to Walk Away

If you find that you're losing focus because the task has too much going on, take a few moments and walk away from it. When you can clear your mind and think clearly once more, then return and continue. If there are too many components to the task, it is easy to get confused and frustrating, making it even harder to focus on what the end result needs to be.

Keep a Clear Mind on What You're Working On
 Knowing what you're doing and what you hope to achieve are great for maintaining focus. Make sure that your work area is free of clutter and that you know what you want to achieve, how you're going to achieve it, and the desired outcome. This will make it easier to continue on in the task with a clear mind.

Don't Open the Door to Distraction

We all know what distracts us. We even invite it to do that. However, distractions are the greatest enemy to focus. When you're working on completing a task, make sure that your known distractions are far away and that you won't stand the chance at finding them while you're working on what you need to do.

Have a Quiet Place

A quiet work area is essential for focus. Some people have to have noise or music to work, and that's fine too. Create the environment that works best for your productivity and use that when you feel that your focus is below where it needs to be. If it's a task that requires you to be elsewhere, keep a clear mind and remind yourself of what you're doing and when you want it to be done.

Take Yourself through the Task

If you can think through what you're doing enough to talk your way through it, you can make sure that you're focused on it. Talking your way through a task is a great way to keep yourself focused on it. Just by making the effort to talk about it, you are thinking about it.

Turn Off Electronics

Cell phones and other electronic devices are often a huge source of distraction. Have you ever found yourself looking at your phone just to make sure you haven't missed a call or a message? Phones are notorious for gaining our attention when we need to be thinking about other things. Try turning off all of the electronics that distract you. This will give your mind the ability to focus on what needs your attention at the moment.

Train Your Brain

It sometimes takes time and energy to get your mind to focus on what needs your attention. This will take you making an effort to train your brain to focus on one task at a time and push everything else out of your mind. When you're working on something, make it a point to ignore everything else around you and focus on your task alone.

Know Your Distractions

Even though you can name a list of things that will distract you, there are things that are distractions that you might not even realize are distracting you. However, if you're alert and looking for distractions as they show up, then you will be more aware of what distracts you and how to avoid it.

For a while, you might want to write down your distractions to remind you that they are indeed distractions. The next time you encounter it, you will see it for what it really is!

There are many elements within our lives that can distract us from what we really need to accomplish. In order to regain your focus, you need to learn how to limit your distractions. When you master how to ignore your distractions, you will find that your mind will be more focused on what you're trying to accomplish. By regaining focus, you will be better able to avoid procrastination and become more motivated and productive. Find what distracts you and make every effort to be focused on what you hope to accomplish.

Chapter 21

Execute with Efficiency

How you execute your "to-do" list is as important as the tasks themselves.

Map out "downtime." Some people advocate using tools that enforce productivity and prioritization. They will argue that the time at your desk needs to be for work and work alone. As you build your day, make sure you have save some down time scheduled. Choose an activity that makes you feel recharged, whether it's playing a video game, reading a romance novel, or going for a jog.

Wean yourself off social media. If you are like the rest of us, and are required to produce some sort of deliverable work on a daily basis, social media will only serve to distract and diminish your time and energy. Yes, this also includes LinkedIn.

Always keep in mind whoever really calls the shots. You may think it's your boss, or your boss' boss, or the "big boss" in the corner office. That's not quite so. For most companies, the boss is the collection of individuals or corporations who buy products and or services. If your work reflects a dedication to helping your clients succeed, you have mastered the art of prioritization.

Set up your own two-minute drill. David Allen referred to this as the two-minute rule and it's been very helpful for me to make sure my priorities are right.

Listen to your body and mind. We often feel compelled to push ourselves beyond the breaking point. This results in fatigue, stress, and sometimes physical breakdown and actual illness. When you feel tired: rest. When you are hungry: eat something. When your mind is wandering: stop what you are doing and take the necessary time to reset. Too many people get hung up on the idea that, while at work, all you should do is work. Instead of falling into that trap, pay attention to the cues your body and mind send you.

Declutter as often as you can. I recommend daily, and think weekly is the bare minimum. That means cleans your desktop, file all your emails in your inbox, and return items that you have borrowed from colleagues. By keeping your desk and computer clean, you give yourself the least stressful environment possible.

Making small changes can help you better prioritize your work. In becoming more productive, you will achieve more, in less time and with less stress. That is, by definition, working smarter.

Chapter 22

Starting Early in Order to Get It All Done

When you're busy, it can be easy to let some tasks just fall through the cracks. If you don't have time, then you cannot do them, right? Well, when you find that you're stuck with the tasks later on, it can be even more frustrating and stressful to get them accomplished. If you would have found the time to do them earlier, then you wouldn't be in a position where you have to rush to get them done right now. How can you make sure that you have time to get everything that you need to get done accomplished?

Time management is a great tool to helping you get more done, but if you're already short on time, then you will find that your efforts at time management might be difficult.

However, waking up earlier and getting an early start can help you to make sure that you're getting it done. In this chapter, we are going to look at how to get an earlier start to get what you need to get done finished.

Set Your Alarm Clock an Hour Earlier

When you lead a busy life, a few extra minutes of sleep seems like paradise. However, by milking sleep early in the morning, you are depriving yourself of time to accomplish your tasks later on in the day. If you were to just wake up one hour earlier than you usually do, you would be able to accomplish much more in the course of a day. What would you do with an extra hour of time? It might make the difference of accomplishing what you set out to do or having to postpone your tasks for another day.

Make Plans to be Active as Soon as You Wake Up
If you're in the habit of sitting down and doing mental work first thing in the morning, you may not be as focused as you could be. Since your brain is still asleep, you might find that your productivity mentally is very much diminished when you first wake up. Try to counteract the effects of waking up by making plans to do something that is active when you first wake up. This can mean working out, going for a walk, or cooking breakfast.

Getting your body moving when you first wake up will help your blood to circulate so that your brain will have the opportunity to wake up before you do any tasks that require thinking.

Eat a Meal that will give you an Energy Boost

Certain foods have the ability to give you the energy you need in order to get going earlier in the day. I'm not saying drink five cups of coffee. This is a temporary fix for an energy boost and you will find that you will crash off of the caffeine high pretty quickly. Try finding foods that are high in protein and minerals that can give you natural energy that will last. This can give you a longer source of energy and not cause a crash later on.

Make Earlier Plans in the Day

If you struggle with waking up early in the morning, then try making plans that will force you to wake up earlier. These can be as simple as making a doctor's appointment at eight in the morning. This will force you to wake up and get out of bed and get going at an earlier hour. Once you have finished your task, then you can get your other, must do tasks out of the way earlier in the day.

Go to Bed Earlier at Night

When people are busy, they tend to stay up later at night to get everything done. By the time that you accomplish what you want to get done, you are so tired that the tasks lack the quality and attention that the task requires. If you were to go to bed earlier and rise earlier in the morning, you would find that the tasks that you wish to accomplish will get done with better quality than if you force yourself to stay awake later in order to finish them.

Get a Restful Sleep

It can be hard to get what you need to get done accomplished if you don't rest well at night. Sometimes it is difficult to fall asleep when you have so much going on in your head. However, the work that your brain does at night prohibits you from getting the rest you need in order to be alert. Make sure that you rest well at night. You may have to drink some herbal tea or take a natural supplement that will help you to fall asleep at night.

Take a Shower to Wake Up

Sometimes, a lukewarm shower can do a wonder in waking you up in the morning. The colder the water, the better it will stimulate you when you first wake up in the morning. Try using this method when you first wake up to see if you can wake up earlier and be more alert first thing in the morning.

There are several methods for waking up earlier in the morning and being more alert in order to get more accomplished. Some work better for people than others, so by finding the ones that work the best for you, you will be able to be more productive and accomplish more in your day.

Chapter 23

Have Goals and Routines to Save Time

When time is scarce, you feel as though you will never be able to accomplish what you want to do each and every day. If you are not in the habit of planning out your day, you might be missing out on some of the work that you need to do. Having a clear plan for your day will allow you to know what you must do next and not have to stop and think about your next step. You can actually save yourself time by having a clear plan before you even set out for the day.

Have a List of Must Dos for the Day

Knowing what you need to get done before you even get started for the day will help you to stay focused and know what you have to do when you are at a loss as to what to do next. By knowing what needs to be done by the end of the day, you are not going to be surprised when you forget to do an important errand. Making this list will only take a few minutes to compile and it will help you to make sure that you're doing what you must throughout the day.

Set Up a Consistent Routine for Your Daily Tasks
A routine may seem overrated, but if you find that you're doing the same things on a daily basis, doing them in a certain order will help you to get them all done without having to think too much about what comes next.

Sometimes, having a routine that you don't have to think much about will be to your benefit. If it comes to the point where you're too busy to think, the routine will help you to carry on with your day.

Set Reasonable Time Limits for Accomplishing Your Tasks
Having a time frame in which you would like to accomplish certain tasks will help you to make sure that they are done during that period of time. However, you really have to make sure that the time limits are reasonable, or you will end up putting too much pressure on yourself and making life more difficult.

Don't Take on Too Many Extra Tasks on a Daily Basis
Sadly, enough, busy people tend to take on much more work than they can possibly handle on a daily basis. When you do this, you will find that you won't get it all done and become frustrated. When planning out your day, only take on what you know you can handle. If you find that you have extra time later on, you can always do more. You will only disappoint yourself if you cannot accomplish everything that you set out to do.

Allow Time for the Unexpected

Life happens and you are powerless to control it. You must be aware of this when things happen that will change the course of your day. When these events happen, you need to be able to roll with it and change your plans to accommodate the unexpected.
By building in a little time for the unexpected around your schedule, you won't be thrown off guard and feel stressed out when it does happen.

Don't Get Upset When Not Everything Gets Accomplished
Life is busy and you're busy. Sometimes, things are going to be left undone. You cannot become upset when this happens. If you find that time does run out, then try to fit in

167

those chores as soon as you can. It's not going to be the end of the world if you don't get everything done the way you planned it. Tomorrow is a new day, and you can always get it done. If you continually become irritated when you fail to finish your plans, then you will be creating undue stress for yourself.

Planning out your day and your routine will help you to manage your time better before you even start it. By having a clear and concise idea of how your day will play out, you will be prepared to move on to the next task without having to think through your actions in detail. Also, having a good routine will help you manage your time better and allow you to get the regular tasks that you work on daily to become natural and automatic for you. Take some time and figure out your day in advance. It could really help your productivity.

Chapter 24

Coming Up with a System to Accomplish Regular Tasks Faster

Since your life is different from anyone else's, it might be difficult to find a definite system and routine to get your day moving smoothly. However, once you find a good fit in routine and a great planning system, you will find that your day will move along flawlessly for the most part. Having a good system to your day will help your time management, your productivity, and will give you the ability to know what is coming next.

Have an Action Plan

The more prepared you are for your day in advance, the easier it will flow as it plays itself out. Having a solid action plan can help you to make the tasks of the day flow without difficulty. If you have a routine that you go through periodically, having that as part of your action plan can make your day start out on an even keel and flow into other tasks that may not be a part of your normal routine. Think through your day before you even begin it and know what you will do and when.
Plan Your Errands so that they are done in an Order That Makes Them Faster

If you have several errands that need to be run in a day, plan them out so that you do them in an order that makes sense and will help you to accomplish them faster. This means that if you are going to multiple places, plan out the tasks so that you go the shortest distance between errands and you won't have to back track to accomplish something later on. For example, if the grocery store and the pet store are close together, plan on making those tasks happen one after another. This will save you time because you're not having to drive longer distances to get back to the pet store if you do something in between.

Try to Accomplish as Much as You Can in One Location Having several tasks that can be taken care of in one location can save you a lot of time and effort. There are many retail stores that specialize in offering multiple goods in one place. If you have to pick up several items, try using one of these stores. For example, you need some groceries along with some sheets for the bed. Going to a store that sells both of these items will save you time and energy.

You won't have to drive elsewhere to accomplish two tasks because they can both be done in the same store.

Have a Clear Idea of What You Will Do Next

When you plan out your busy day well, you will always have a clear idea of what should be done next. Having a clear idea of what you will do when will help you to allow your day to flow without wasting time planning out your next move. The great thing about doing this is that it only takes a few minutes in the morning to plan out an entire day. Even if something comes up and you have to change your plans, you won't feel as confused by the changes if you are able to jump right back into the plans you have for the day.

Don't Let Obstacles Faze You

Life is full of obstacles and everything that we plan on doing in a given day may not go as we have planned. For some people, this can cause a ton of stress. When people stress out, the rest of the day tends to fall apart. So, when something does come up and your day doesn't go as you have planned, don't let the changes faze you. Allow them to roll and keep on trying to do your best to fall back into the plan that you set up that morning. If you don't stress over the inevitable, your mind will adjust and you can move on throughout the rest of the day more easily.

Allow others to help if it is offered

If you have a regular routine and you find that something has come up, allow others to help you to get your day back on track. This could be as simple as having someone photocopy the reports that you plan on using in a meeting later in the day. This is a task that needs to be done and someone else can easily help you to accomplish it while you find ways to get your schedule back on track.

Be Prepared for Anything

Since life is often unpredictable, being prepared for things that may happen will help you roll with the punches a little better. If you have a clear and concise plan for your day and you find that it's not going as planned, you may find yourself frustrated and stressed out, making the rest of your day seem like a total failure. Don't allow the unplanned to ruin your day. Take it in stride and do your best to work around it.

Having an approach to help you with your day and the unexpected can make your life much easier. Allowing for the unplanned will make it easier for you to get your day back on track and still be able to do what you originally planned to do. Having systems that will allow you to work around life's obstacles will help you to become a more productive and less stressed out individual.

Chapter 25

Structuring Your Time for Productivity

No matter how hard you try, there will always only be twenty-four hours in a given day. There is no way to make a day longer or shorter, so don't even try wishing for that to happen. The one thing that you can do to be more productive is structure the time you do have so that you can accomplish more. There are multiple ways to accomplish this. Depending on your situation, you might find that you can structure your time using one method much better than you can using another.

Having a structure for your time will help you to be much more productive and to get what you need to accomplish done. You don't necessarily have to put yourself on a strict schedule in order to structure your time effectively. I'm going to give you some tips on how to structure your time better in order to have an opportunity to accomplish all of your given tasks.

Have Blocks of Time Set Aside for Certain Tasks

Successful people have times where they will do certain tasks. It might help to purchase a day planner that has a daily breakdown of time so that you can block out your time and make certain times for certain projects. This will give you a visual representation of what your day will look like before you even begin. Also, it will help you to plan out the rest of your day without having to second guess your schedule. This will save you the embarrassment of taking on too much in the course of a day.

Make Your Schedule as Regular as You Possibly Can

Having a routine and regular schedule will help your mind and body adjust to life's demands. Try getting your schedule regular and keeping it that way. This may mean that you work regular hours and that you do certain errands on certain days of the week at certain times. Knowing what you can expect next will help you to make sure that you're accomplishing your goals without stressing yourself out.

Know Your Habits and Your Day as Well as You Can

If you have habits that will prevent you from being productive, knowing what prevents your productivity will help you to overcome your bad habits. The more that you resist your bad habits, the easier it will be to break yourself of that bad habit. If you know your habits and your day well, then you will be able to plan around them to make your day as productive as you possibly can.

Don't Procrastinate

Procrastination is a bad habit to be in and getting what you need to do done at the last possible minute will not only affect the quality of the task, but it will also stress you out because you are going to feel the pressure to get it done quickly. By planning on getting what you need to do done thoroughly to begin with and allowing yourself enough time to accomplish it, you can avoid quality issues and undue stress. Make it a habit to give yourself enough time to finish everything without waiting until the last possible moment.

Leave Some Time in Your Schedule to Relax

If your schedule is back to back errands, you are going to burn out. You need to build time into your schedule to relax and do things that you enjoy. Plan time for yourself in your busy schedule and make sure that you take care of yourself and your needs. That will help you to be relaxed and prepared to do whatever else needs to be done. Even if you feel like you have too much to do to relax, make it a priority and don't allow your life to stress you out.

Don't Allow Your Schedule to be Thrown Too off Course

When unexpected things happen to you, don't allow it to throw your day and your schedule too off course. If you allow things to affect you in such ways, you may have a hard time recovering from the unexpected and getting your life back on track. Depending on how busy you are, this can have a drastic domino effect, making it so that your entire week is thrown off. When that happens, you will feel stressed out and that will affect your health and your mood.

Try getting your day back on track as soon as you can, even if it means changing some plans.

Have the Tools You Need in Order to Get the Job Done

Right the First Time

Knowing what resources are needed in order to do what needs to be done is incredibly important to saving time and getting it done right the first time and not having to search to get the right tools for the job. Plan ahead well enough so that you have what you need to do what you need to do the task the right the first time.

Having a great way to structure your time and your tasks will help you to get what needs to be done more quickly and efficiently. The better that you know your day and what your schedule requires will help you to be a more productive individual, even if your life feels incredibly busy. Make yourself a structure and do your best to keep with it. It will help you to accomplish all that you want to within a given day.

Chapter 26

Structuring Your Schedule to Get More Done in Less Time

Having a schedule with a nice structure will help you to get more out of your day and help you to accomplish what needs to be done in a smaller amount of time. In the last chapter, we covered how to structure your day and not fall into bad habits. Structuring your tasks will help you to make more time in your schedule for relaxation and others.

Knowing how your day will play out and how your tasks will play out will help you to structure the tasks to be done in an organized manner. By taking time to get your tasks planned into your schedule and structuring your tasks in order to achieve them faster, you will find that you will have more time than you thought that you did!

Have a Systematic Approach to Your Tasks

Using a system to plan your tasks can help you to focus on getting them done in a timely and productive manner.

When I talk about a systematic approach, I mean that you perform the task the same way repeatedly. Finding out how to accomplish this the best will help you to get it done quickly and be able to move on to what you have planned next. Depending on how familiar you are with you schedule and your tasks, you can focus on ways to save time while you're working on getting your to do list finished.

Learning How to Accomplish the Task in a Structured Manner

Performing a task in a structured manner is much like having a systematic approach to it, but it differs in the sense that you focus on how to do that task the best and in the fastest manner. This breaks down the tasks into smaller parts so that you can get each portion done quickly and efficiently. Since each individual task is different, it may take some time to break down a task to make it go faster.

When learning how to accomplish tasks in a more structured manner, focus on tasks that you do on a regular basis and get in the habit of using this approach.
Making Goals to Do Certain Tasks as Quickly as Possible Without Compromising Quality
Sometimes when you do a task quickly to save time, it will lack in quality.

You want to be able to do whatever you set out to do quickly without harming the overall quality of the overall result. When you're focusing on speed, rather than focus directly on the end result, focus on the steps that will take you to that result and how you can make those steps faster. If you continue to focus on the individual parts rather than the end result, the quality of the finished product will still be top notch.

Plan Similar Types of Tasks to be performed in the Same Time Period
If your to do list calls for similar tasks that need to be done, group them together so that you can do them at the same time. This can be accomplished for a number of circumstances surrounding the task, such as location, difficulty level, or what is required of the task. If several tasks require that you make a phone call, try to set aside some time to make all of your phone calls during the same time period. This will help you to get that particular chore done without spreading it out into different time slots.

Think of ways that you can group your tasks together to be able to accomplish them during the same time period and ultimately save you time.

If Your Tasks Take You to Certain Areas, Plan Your Route so that You're Traveling the Shortest Distance

If you live in a city where there are different places that you need to go, try planning out a travel route in between the places that you need to go so that you are going the shortest distance and you can get the chores done in these locations done in the quickest manner possible. It is senseless to bounce back and forth to locations that you could have visited when doing another chore or errand. Think through your route before you leave your home and make it as short as you possibly can.

Having structure in your tasks and doing them in such a way that will save you time and extra effort will help you to get them done faster. Try thinking of ways that you can break down your tasks and your schedule in order to fit more into it within a shorter time frame. By making the best use of your time and your skills, you can get more done in less time and have more time to do whatever you enjoy doing.

Chapter 27

Manage your time properly

If you're easily distracted and that leads to not being able to get important tasks done until the very last moment, then you have a time management problem as well. Don't worry, many people struggle with time management skills. However, knowing that you are struggling with it and doing something about it are two entirely different things.

At the end of the day, you might realize that you wasted a lot of time that could have been used for productivity. In hindsight, you're kicking yourself for not putting down the remote and cleaning that kitchen. However, that time is long gone now and you have to allot another time period to that task. Which means another task gets pushed back? It can be a vicious and frustrating cycle.

Time management isn't about micromanaging your day. It's about setting up a loose time frame on the task you're doing. By saying that you wish to do this task in a certain time frame, you tend to manage that time more precisely so that you can meet your goal. In this chapter, I'm going to give you some tips on enhancing your time management skills.

Give Yourself a Sufficient Amount of Time to Complete a Task

If you feel like you're in a time crunch, then you will feel like it might be better to put the task aside until later. By giving yourself enough time to complete the task, you will be better able to get it done and out of the way.

Don't Try and be a Super Hero

Don't try and take on too many projects or chores. You're only human, and by trying to be a super hero, you're preparing yourself for being burnt out fast. Take only what you can handle and let others help with the rest.

Have Your Day Loosely Planned

By knowing what you plan to do and roughly when, you can easily fit in other tasks along the way. So, if you need to get gas, try stopping at a station that is near the grocery store so that you can pick up the eggs you need for that recipe!

Work on One Task at a Time

You hear employers talk about multitasking. While it seems like a good idea, it can often be damaging to your overall performance. If you're focused on more than one project at a time, things are not going to get done as completely as if you were only focusing on one. So, take your tasks one at a time and see how much better they get accomplished!

Have What You Need to Complete Your Task

It's just a waste of time if you have to leave mid task to go and find an item that is necessary for its completion. Before you even begin your project, make sure that you have everything and enough of everything. That way, you don't find yourself in the frustrating situation of having to run out to get something mid-work.

Consolidate Steps

If something can be made easier by streamlining it, do it. Make your steps as concise as possible and it will make the

179

project work much better in the end. However, if there isn't a way to cut corners, don't. You don't want the quality of your work to suffer.

Do the Hard Part First?

You will find that if you do the difficult part of the task first that everything else will fall into place around it. Try this the next time you feel like you will never get through your tasks. It will help you to get the intimidating part out of the way and make the rest seem easy.

Stay Focused

Focus is the main tool to making sure that you're completing your tasks efficiently and in a timely manner. Take some tips from how to stay focused and see how well they can help you to become more productive.

Make the Best Use of Your Time

If you have free time on your hands, don't waste it. Find great uses for it that are productive and will be helpful in the long run.

Managing your time well is the key to making sure that you get what you want to accomplish done. Those who procrastinate tend to have poor time management skills, making it difficult for them to be productive. If you have a time management problem, seek ways to use your time better and more efficiently. It will help in the long run!

Chapter 28

Finding Balance and Managing Your Day

The dreaded to do list. It needs done, but it's just a hassle that you wish you could burn. If you could do everything on it in minutes, it wouldn't seem like such a nuisance, but that will never happen. So, how can you make that list seem not so intimidating and still feel like you have a life?

Balance is a key element to any situation. You want to get important tasks done, but you also don't want to be working twenty-four hours a day. However, if you learn to manage your time and not procrastinate, that to do list might not be as annoying as it would be if you're trying to do it all at the end of your day.

Choosing the Most Important Tasks First

I'm just going to come out and say it-we fill our lives with junk. Some of the activities we pursue are often unnecessary and not pertinent to our lives. When you set out to do errands, pick the tasks that are necessary first and then go from there. If you find that you don't have time to accomplish the tasks at the end of your list, you're not missing the most important elements of your day!

Letting Stuff Wait When it is Not Needed Right Away
Now, I'm not telling you to procrastinate! I'm just saying to evaluate what needs to be done immediately and what can wait until a later time. Once you find a good time to do something, then do it. Don't put it off until later when there is no reason to not do it at that moment. However, if you have a long list of tasks, put the less pertinent tasks towards the bottom.

Splitting Up the Work

If you have many people in your household or office, make it a team effort. Some people take on all of the work and that can easily overwhelm and burn them out. So, find a way to delegate these tasks so that they don't all fall on you.

Making Time for You

It sounds selfish, but you really do need to have some time that is solely yours. This is time to make sure that you get your rest and do activities that you enjoy. By taking a break from the constant struggles of life, you will be prepared to tackle your chores without the lag of someone who is burnt out and ready to throw in the towel.

Reward Yourself

While you're in the middle of your day, take a little time to give yourself a reward for the hard work that you've already accomplished. This can be a piece of candy or a cup of coffee from your favorite café. Find something that will motivate you to continue on with the day. Think of it as a way to motivate yourself to be more productive and not just stop where you are and call it quits!

Don't Put Too Much Pressure on Yourself

Don't put too much pressure on yourself. It will only make you more nervous and less likely to want to pursue the project to begin with. As long as you do your best with what you have, let that be your reward. Going above and beyond is great at times, but if that's how you operate on everything, then you're going to be disappointed often. Not only that, but you're going to burn yourself out on life.

Know Your Limits

There is a time in everyone's life where enough is enough. You are human and there is only so much you can take on. If it gets to the point where you're not getting anything out of life for yourself, then you've gone way past your limits and that is a sure sign that you need to back up and reevaluate your priorities. It sounds selfish, but you do need to look out for yourself and your needs. If you find that you have too much to do and no time to breathe, cut some of the tasks from your day so that you're not stretching yourself too thin.

Learn to Say No

This tip goes hand in hand with the last one. If people see that you're willing to do anything for them, they will begin to take advantage of that. This only makes it harder on you and easier on them. So, if you notice that a certain person tends to push work off on you, learn to say no to them. You don't have to be blunt when doing this. Just kindly say that you don't have time for that right now and cannot take it on. If that person truly respects you, they will understand that you're looking out for yourself.

Don't make it Harder on Yourself

Having a balance in your life is essential to making sure that you're accomplishing what needs to be done and not going overboard with the outcome. Even if you're the type of person who will give everything 110 percent of your efforts, realize that it's okay to not be perfect all the time. Know what needs that extra effort and what just needs to be done.

Chapter 29

Learning How to Manage Tasks

Force Yourself to Do It
Sometimes we have to buckle down and just do it. We don't
want to and the motivation simply is not there. However, just
jumping in and getting it done prevents us from
procrastinating it and it gets done. It's kind of like eating
your vegetables. You don't want to but you force them down
anyway!

Write Down Your Approach before You Begin

If you're one of those people who have no idea where you
will start on something, try doing it this way. Think through
how you will go about the project and each step that you
plan to take along the way. Once you have a solid idea as to
an approach, put that into action. You will be surprised at
how well your task is falling together when you have a
definite plan for it!

Integrate the Task into Your Day

If the task that you're pursuing is something that needs to be
done frequently, such as washing the clothes, make it a part
of your daily schedule. If you plan a time and a place for it,
then it must get done then.

Use Techniques that Have Worked in the Past

I'm sure that everyone has times in their lives where they
were super motivated and everything just seemed to fall into
place. Think back to those times and think about what made
that work. Was it attitude? Or was it the fact that you

enjoyed seeing your productivity? Think about what made those tasks flow into your day and try those techniques in order to make them do so once more. What works in the past often will work again?

Take Advice from Others

If you know of people who do the same types of tasks regularly and seem to be very good at completing them, ask them for their advice. People love to be asked about something that they are perceived to do well at. They will even offer additional information that might be helpful as well. Use this as a tool to help you with your motivation and drive to complete the project or task. Someone might just have a great idea that will work great for you. You don't know unless you take the time to ask!

Try New Methods of Doing Chores

If it's monotony the makes you procrastinate a task, try a different approach to it. Let me use the laundry example again. You hate doing laundry because it's a long and tedious task that sucks your time down the toilet. Why not try pairing laundry with another activity and accomplishing both at the same time? You don't have to be present at all times while doing laundry, so maybe you can work on cleaning the family room while your clothes are in the dryer and when they come out, you will be ready to fold them.

There are many different tasks within a daily life can be altered so that you're more productive and getting it done more efficiently. It just takes a little creativity on your part to ensure that you think through it before making the effort.
Have a Positive Attitude
The way that you look at and perceive something will ultimately tell you how well you will accomplish it. If you feel

negatively about the task from the beginning, it will be a negative and grueling task for you this time and every time. So, try and take a look at the task in a different light.

Think of something good that can come from it. For example, when you finish your laundry, you will have clean clothes and your house will look tidier. Just little positive notes on a task can make it seem like a nicer one when you complete it.

Sometimes the reasons that we don't like to do things is because we don't manage the tasks correctly. It can be anything from our approach to the project to the way we visualize it as being a pain. Whatever reason keeps you procrastinating a project, try to view it in a different light and see how much more productive you really can be. Your approach can have a great effect on how you do the project and how timely the project is done.

Try different approaches to your tasks and see if there are ways to make them work more efficiently for you. Even if you feel like a task is just okay, play with it a little bit. If nothing else works out, the go back to the old way. Keep on trying different methods and see what can work for you!

Chapter 30

Enjoying a Motivated and Productive Life

Procrastinating is one of the worst habits a productive person can develop. Everyone has a reason for why they put things off, but in the end, it's all the same. We've procrastinated and now we're forced to complete that task in record time. If only we had thought of this when we first knew it had to be done...

Enjoying life isn't necessarily about having free time and being great at everything. It's about disciplining yourself and making it a point to improve on your weak points. Some people are content with the way they are. Good for them.

In order to enjoy your life as being motivated and productive, you must learn to put the procrastination habit on the shelf and leave it there to rot. It's not easy. If you're used to putting aside tasks until you feel like doing them, making yourself do them right away is going to feel uncomfortable for a while. Once you get into the habit, you will find that you enjoy being productive and laugh at yourself for the times when you would procrastinate it.

Not only will you enjoy being productive and managing your time well, but others will notice the difference in you. You will find that you're more relaxed and not feel pressured by large amounts of work. It will all come with time. You're not going to be able to change years of habits overnight.

Just remember, procrastination leads to stress, and stress leads to a less enjoyable life. Just because you're intimidated by the list of tasks before you, don't make the situation worse by procrastinating them. Take some of the tips that I've mentioned and make yourself face your struggle head on.

Once you've found a balance between time management and focus, you will notice that your tendency to procrastinate has gone way down. Great job. Continue to build healthy time management habits so that you won't fall into the trap of procrastination again.
It's not an easy struggle to overcome, but if you're determined, it will all come together in due time. Just keep at it!

Motivating Yourself in the Morning

If you're like a lot of people, you tend to look at yourself in the mirror first thing in the morning. You either note how horrible you look or you already have a plan for how you're going to shape your look for the rest of the day.

A Boost of Energy

Everything is good in moderation. However, if you find that you're dependent on caffeine to keep you going during the day, you need to evaluate a healthier approach to finding energy during the day.

People who are more self-disciplined tend to be more successful at whatever they put their minds to. It's tough to keep yourself in line sometimes. Everyone has their temptations and vices that will make them stray from their ultimate goals. However, being disciplined will help you define your limits and know when you're getting out of line with your goals and expectations. So, when you find that you have no self-discipline, try to find ways to build that discipline and keep it strong whenever you see an opportunity to stray.

Plan a Routine

Having a plan and sticking to a plan is a great method for keeping yourself disciplined. It takes some time to get a productive routine down, but once you have it, it's a quick way to ensure that you are disciplined and staying motivated throughout the day.

Keep to Your Routine as Closely as Possible

Life has a funny way of interrupting our best laid plans. However, it's how we handle life's distractions that will make us successful. So, when you find that something is interrupting your routine, get past it as soon as possible and carry on with your routine as if it didn't happen. By sticking by your routine, you will be more likely to keep the momentum of your day going in high gear.

Have the Same Routine Daily

It can get incredibly confusing if you change your routine too often. Have one routine and work towards keeping it consistent from day to day. A routine can help you continue a consistent flow throughout your day. It might take a little bit to get your routine into place, but once you do, you will be well on your way to having a driving force that will propel you through the day.

Have Specific Goals

Goals are an important part of motivation. If you don't know what you're aiming for, then you basically walking in circles. So, have specific goals for whatever you would like to achieve in place before you go for it. By knowing what you want and what you expect to gain from the activity will make you more motivated to give it your complete and total effort.

Design Your Life to Fit Around Your Goals

Knowing what you want to accomplish is a good factor to motivate you to succeed in achieving it. So, once you know what you want and what your goals are for the outcome, structure your activities around the goal. This can be simply telling yourself that you want to be at this place at this specific time.

Organize Your Day

Self-discipline can be a difficult area to cultivate. We are our toughest critics, but we are also the first ones to throw in the towel when life gets tough. By taking a few moments to but these hacks into practice, you can keep yourself on track and stay productive and motivated no matter what the circumstances might be.

Chapter 31

Creating Personal Success

Everyone wants to be successful. Whether it be at a job or at a specific task, we want to have something to show for our efforts. Whatever you want to pursue as your personal success, put your full efforts towards it and don't give up on it. I'm going to suggest some hacks that will help you to boost your own personal success and help you to continue on to becoming an overall successful person.

Have a Plan

In order to be successful, you need to know what you want and how you plan to accomplish it. Be specific. What do you want, and what will it take for you to get to that point of achieving it? Ask yourself these questions. Know exactly what you're aiming for before you even begin. After you know what you want, then plan on how you're going to get there. For example, you have decided that you want to own your own home, but you don't have the necessary funds to put a down payment down on the type of home that you want. So, how will you be successful in your goal? Well, you decide that you're going to take on a second job in order to raise the money to make a decent down payment. Once you have that money, then you will continue your search for your own home. You know what you want and you have a plan to achieve that goal.

Know Your Opponents

No matter what you have planned, there will be people and other circumstance that will stand in your way. By knowing what these are, you stand a better chance at getting through these obstacles when the approach you. Going back to our example about purchasing a home, you find that your boss doesn't like you and cuts your hours so that you're not making much money. This is an opponent to your goal. Do whatever is necessary to sidestep this and continue toward your goal. It might be finding a different job or moving to a different area of the business. Find a good solution to get around this opponent.

Know Your Obstacles

Just like you will have opponents, you will also face unknown obstacles in your journey towards your goal. Your car breaks down and you have to invest in a new one, which takes some of the money you had saved for the down payment for your home. These are just minor setbacks that will make your goal seem further away. Recognize an obstacle when it arises and rise above it so it doesn't stop you from what you want to achieve.

Have a Driving Force

There is always something that is a force behind what we do. In the example of the house, the driving force might be the start of a family. You want a family badly, but you don't want to have one until you are stable and settled. Knowing what you want from the goal will help you to keep pursuing it, no matter how difficult it gets.

Stay Determined

If you lose your passion for what you're working towards, then you will lose the desire to keep on going. Stay determined and keep focused on the end goal. By having that focus and determination, you're allowing yourself the opportunity to succeed.

Don't Let Anyone Discourage You

There is always going to be someone out there who is going to mock and criticize your efforts. What you do with this treatment will ultimately determine your success. If you truly want what you're working towards, then don't let what anyone says discourage your efforts. What you ultimately let yourself believe can influence the final outcome of your goals and plans. Let yourself believe in your success and don't allow anyone else to stand in the way.

Fight for What You Want

Sometimes, you're going to be the only one who will be fighting for what you want. People might laugh and mock you for your efforts, but in the end, what you fight for is up to you. If you have a dream, don't let other people's opinions dictate how the outcome will look like. Be determined and motivated for what you want and not let anyone stand in your way.

Success is tough for some and it comes easily for others. Whatever success looks like for you, know what you want and what stands in your way to achievement. Be willing to go the extra mile and make the extra effort to succeed in whatever you set out to achieve.

Chapter 32

Building a More Motivated and Successful You

In the end, you are the one who controls whether or not you find success or failure. Sadly, enough, many people set themselves back by having a negative self-image or outlook on their present situation. You might be one of those people who doesn't believe that you can ever be motivated or successful. Change that mindset! Every person on this earth is capable of achieving much more than they think! So, take some time and know what you want and what motivates you to achieve your goals.

You can be your best friend or your worst critic. It's ultimately up to you. So, the first decision that you must make is whether or not you're going to allow yourself to be set back or if you're not going to let anything stand in your way. Once you have made that decision, then you're ready to move on to the next phase. Hopefully, you chose not to let anything stand in your way. Let that be your mantra when times get rough. Just keep going....

Once you have a more positive and affirmative self-image, you will be ready to set goals and find success. Don't get me wrong, success can be difficult to achieve. However, your motivation and efforts make a world of difference when it comes to achieving the desired end result. Being a positive and encouraging resource to yourself is a key to ensuring your overall success. If you cannot find that positivity, find ways to find it. It might be friends, it might be a church group, or it might just come to you in a quiet moment. Once you find it, hold tight to it.

Success is something that everyone strives for their entire lives. However, many set themselves back by picking up bad habits and allowing themselves to limit their personal possibilities. Don't set yourself back in this way. If you find that you're a negative person, find ways to make your mindset positive. There is something out there for everyone. It might not be what you planned, but it will still be just right for you.

Don't let time be an excuse for your failure. By using a few simple hacks, you can make a great difference in the way you use your time and build your motivation. I'm giving my ideas to you as a tool to help you to become a better you.

Take whatever is useful to you and use it to your advantage. I wish you all the luck and success that there is to be found in your life! You can do this! Don't let anything set you back!

Coming Up with Methods to make your job easier

Chores Easier

The greatest part about our society is that there are creative people who are constantly coming up with new inventions to make lives easier. Don't think of these inventions as an excuse to be lazy, but rather, look at them as an opportunity to get more accomplished faster. Not only are there great inventions to help you with your life, but you can also come up with hacks and other methods to make what must be done easier and less time consuming.

Use Tools that Make the Job Easier

We may make fun of people for some of the ideas that they try to market, but some of the tools really do make life easier. Try taking some of these tools and making them work for whatever you're working on at the time. If you're in charge of cooking a meal, try using the microwave tools that will help you to accomplish the same quality of product without as much hassle. If you find that you do some tasks more often than others, find tasks that will help you to get them done faster with the same quality.

Learn Tricks to Getting Tasks Done from Others

People are constantly finding creative ways to get what you want to accomplish done faster. It can really benefit you to take a look at some of these tips and try using them when you're trying to accomplish tasks of your own. There are numerous websites that offer advice and hacks on how to do common household tasks in different ways that you may not have thought about.

Look for Ways to Cut Corners without Cutting Quality

You may think that cutting corners on a project can harm the quality of the end result, but there are ways to do this without compromising the quality. Find ways to cut corners in your common tasks so that you can get the job done faster. If you find that cutting corners cuts quality, find other ways to make the task easier. It may take time to figure out what works and what doesn't

Be Creative and Find Ways to Make the Task Easier

The inventors of random inventions are not the only ones who can be creative when it comes to making life easier. You may have ideas on how to make your common tasks easier and they may not be in conventional ways. Use your creativity and get your tasks done faster. Don't be afraid to try new things even if they sound insane. Some of the best inventions have come from seemingly crazy ideas!

Take the Advice of Others and Try it

The great part about family and friends is that they have a
wealth of tips and advice to make life easier. Don't be afraid
to try some of this advice to make your own life easier. Some
of it may work for you, while other bits of advice might be
totally useless. The point is that you won't know if it's useful
or not unless you give it a try!

Finding ways to make your common tasks quicker and easier
will open up more free time for you. If you're a busy person,
having time for yourself is a treat. By learning how to make
your life easier, you can find more time for yourself and lean
to enjoy that time more often.

Chapter 33

Finding a Routine and Sticking to It

Routines are the best method to making a busy life seem simpler and more productive. Everyone has routines of some sort, whether it be how they prepare themselves for the world in the morning to how they load their car after a shopping trip. Think of some of the routines that you practice regularly. Now, think about areas of your life where you can use more routine.

By taking the time to build routines in your life, you will stand a better chance at making your life easier and more productive. The times where you felt as though you had no time at all can be a thing of the past. Try building normal and productive routines for your life will help you to realize more relaxing times for yourself. Busy people often tend to be the most disorganized, making it more difficult to have the free time that they desire.

From taking measures to wake up earlier on a daily basis to structuring your schedule, finding ways to make your life productive will help you to live a more fulfilling life. You may think that you will never find a chance to change what you need to in order to find free time within your personal life. Don't be deceived by that lie. You can make your life what you want and if you are set on getting a routine and finding ways to be more productive, you can accomplish whatever you wish to do.

Know your habits and find ways to work around them. By understanding yourself and your schedule, you will be more successful in finding ways to deal with your busy life. Busy doesn't have to be a prison sentence. You can still have a full and enjoyable life, even if you have a million things on your to do list. It's just a matter of finding ways to make your life and your schedule easier to endure.

No matter what, the journey will start with the will power to make changes in your life. If you really want to be more productive and find that free time you want and still get everything done, then it is essential that you learn to manage your time and make your tasks easier to accomplish. The journey starts with you, so you are the one who has to take the first step. Are you ready to be more productive and have more time for what you want to do? Then take the first step!

Life is busy and nothing will change that. How you deal with it will be how you learn to enjoy your life!

Habits to Avoid in Order to become more Productive

In the opening chapter of the book, or the introduction, I talked about perfectionism and also about fear of failure. The psychological approach that you have toward your life in general and toward your work dictates the outcome. The world isn't perfect. Thus, if you are a perfectionist and expect everything to be done in a certain way, chances are you will be very disappointed because life doesn't work like that.

Perfectionism

When you are a perfectionist, you waste time because you are too busy thinking of the theory of doing a job rather than doing it. You also have unreasonable expectations of people who work with you. Unless you can drop this perfectionism, it gets in the way of productivity. Nothing you do is ever good enough and even when you learn new approaches to work, chances are that you will find fault because that's what perfectionists do. They plan to do things but rarely achieve them. In fact, some don't even start their work because their perfectionism stops them in their tracks. Look at it logically, if you expect perfection, you are going to be very disappointed in life. Sometimes, you can achieve good results but the motivation for doing so should not be perfectionism. It should be flexibility in approach and ability to work with others.

More often than not perfectionists have an unrealistic picture of what needs to be done and this needs to be put into perspective. If you suspect that you are putting off work because of perfectionism, you need to ask yourself the following questions:
Does perfectionism get in the way of productivity?
Does perfectionism make you afraid of failure?
The answer to both of these is probably "yes." Thus, you need to accept that life isn't perfect and start to break your work down into manageable proportions without taking your analysis too far. You spend more time analyzing than actually doing. Look at your list of things that you have to do today and see how many of them you have detailed.

Now write yourself another list, merely telling you what the job is and how long you think you should give to that task. Make a point of aiming your perfectionism toward accurate ability to judge how long a job takes. This will give you the incentive to prove yourself right and this may just be the kick that you need in order to perform. Stop working out all of the nitty gritty and start doing the job to the best of your ability.

Stop expecting people around you to adhere to your perfectionist standards because you will alienate people and

make them less motivated to produce or to achieve. There's nothing worse than working for a perfectionist.
Try giving praise where it is due when people help you to achieve goals.

Being afraid of failure

This aspect of non-achievement is huge. You would be surprised how many people don't achieve because they don't even try. They are afraid of failure but what failure is isn't as bad as everyone makes out. Failure acts as a lesson and when you make a mistake, you need to change your attitude. Stop recoiling into your shell and use the mistake to learn from. It isn't that you:
Failed to do the job properly

It is that you:
Learned how not to do the job, so that you know better for your next attempt
Richard Branson, the multi-millionaire owner of the Virgin group of companies was asked once about whether he had ever failed. He laughed at the question and told the reporter that he fails all the time, but that's how he learns and how he makes new discoveries in the future – by avoiding the same action. You can do the same thing too. Stop letting fear hold you back. It's not healthy.

Chapter 34

Growth, Mindset and Ending Bad Habits

And similarly, it's equally essential to be inclined to be uncomfortable and to undergo hardship. How would you lose weight if you are terrified of dieting? How can you expect you'll advance in your job if you shy away from hard work?

However, this really is the reality for many folks. We are only willing to accomplish things that we do not want to do, to install with hard times. We've come to be acutely feeble and it's ultimately making us miserable.

Why We Are Weak

Consider carefully your dog and compare these to a wolf, look at the differences. Your puppy may be loving, fun and loyal but it's solely dependent on you personally. It cannot survive each day in the real world; also it's undoubtedly not a warrior like the wolf is.

Why? Because it's been domesticated, and my good friend, this how you have been conditioned as well.

We haven't become domesticated in the sense of a pet, but we also have gotten lazy, spoiled and too indulged. In society, what's disposable, what comes easily and we no more willpower to wait for anything, everything is at out fingertips. Hungry? Get a takeaway, want entertainment? Surf the web or Facebook. Horny? Okay, go online and voila instant satisfaction. Bored? Turn on the TV and chuckle at comedies. Desire advice? Merely question Siri or ask "Google" on your smart phone. Want to acquire into much better shape? Maybe not, that requires too much out of you.

Being constantly indulged in anything we want, we think it is tougher than to put in any effort for what we really want. Exactly why would we put in effort once we are able to have so much, so easily? And when we have been conditioned to thinking we can have whatever we like at any given moment, we become confused, bored, aloof and impersonal towards others. This is a vicious cycle we must break if we are to achieve greatness and mental toughness in life.

In the past, simply finding food or eating could have required hunting or foraging from sunlight till sundown while trying to stay away from predators. You might be a lot stronger and a lot rougher -- emotionally and physically. However, nowadays we have no drive; we are fatter than ever, lazier, and sicker than ever before in the history of mankind even with the best medicines and doctors money can buy.

Ways to Get Tough

So with this in mind, just how would you really go about becoming tough?
First, you ought to decide to try and live with much less. That means travelling and staying in hostels, or getting a hotel room alone in a faraway land not booking accommodations the night ahead, only carrying a couple outfits.

And in fact, when matters fail, it produces strength and makes it possible to cultivate a more robust and tougher version of you.

Mindset and Growth

So that's an integral purpose really: to continue to keep a growth mindset whatsoever the moments. Each battle which comes your way would be an opportunity to secure tougher and better challenges that lay ahead and you then become smarter. By addressing those hardships, your life gets greater motive (daily life is more futile even if it is effortless) and also you become better armed to take on similar challenges that lie ahead. So, the next time you find yourself in debt, then instead of letting this defeat you, instead, view it as a struggle to overcome, a challenge.

How would you earn the money which takes you out of this? How can you be much better? Do not wallow in worry or anxiety -- that helps no one. See it being a possibility to cultivate and to prevent this taking place and take the crucial actions. Don't be concerned about the way that it seems to be to others, but don't blame yourself for allowing yourself to be in this situation. Just take action and learn from it. You were not adequate enough before, but now you are likely to become improved. In fact, challenge and growth are things that the brain is actually wired for. We thrive if we are challenged mentally and physically, and this leads in the production of hormones like dopamine, and brain derived neurotropic factor and more which help keep us to protect our brains in to older age.

Perhaps you should welcome the issues that come; you also ought to seek them out. Never run from anything or anyone. Throughout days of calmness, you need to put together yourself for battle by learning (looking at books embracing new knowledge) and by training your entire body.

Priorities

Plan out your day
It's all too easy to write a never ending to do list, continually crossing things off and adding a few more. It can feel like a conveyor belt, where each day feels like a repeat of the last, and quite frankly it's exhausting. Is this how anyone wants to live? I highly doubt it.

When we write those kind of lists we often add everything we can think of to them. Every little (and not so little) outstanding task goes on, and we feel good about having it all in one place for all of five minutes before the realization kicks in that we're actually supposed to do it all.

Once you start to feel a sense of doom about a to do list, your chances of looking at it and tackling the things on their fall. It's easier to put your head in the sand than open it and feel like a failure for having 136 uncompleted tasks, right? Of course. It's actually quite unkind to ourselves, because we're bound to feel weighed down by the sheer volume of tasks and that won't help us be more productive.

I'm not saying there isn't a place for this kind of list. If it helps you to remember all the things that you need to do, then that's OK, keep some kind of "master list."

Top 3 priorities

I recommend giving your day some thought ahead of time and allocating just 3 top priorities to each day. You can take these from your master list, your memory or from what didn't get finished yesterday, it doesn't matter, but plan as you go. That way you're not committed to tasks that have been superseded, or aren't essential that day. You can choose these priorities in the morning, or perhaps you'd prefer to end your work day by committing to what you'll do the following morning. It only matters that your system works for you.

Sure, you may have a lot more than 3 things that need to get done in a day, and I know the feeling.

The reality is that not everything is urgent. Checking emails, responding to texts, giving your head of department the data they asked for this morning that isn't actually due until next week. We do it to ourselves and we have it done to us, either out of poor planning, distraction or plain old confusion. Sadly we often don't value other people's time the way we value our own. When you think about what you really must do today, and give yourself 3 things to finalize be the end of the day, you're effectively saying "no" to all of the extraneous demands that get placed upon you, and you're making your own choices instead. You can politely tell your colleague that they'll have the data before their Wednesday deadline but that today you're working on a project that is due in at 5pm today. Simple.

When you choose those 3 priorities for the day, really think about what's going to move you forwards. They might not always be the most fun or the easiest of tasks, but pick the ones that will make the biggest difference to you and where you want to get to. If you start committing to doing that on a regular basis, you will speed towards your goals.

Allocate time to your priorities

Adding a time to each task will focus your efforts far beyond the general scope of the idea, and so is best used when you're feeling as though there just aren't enough hours in the day or you are feeling unfocused.

This works equally well when you split up your day to work on bigger projects, like below, or smaller things in the second example. Adding in a bit of time in your day to catch up on other tasks and tie up loose ends gives you the reassurance that you won't have spent all of your time working on your list. This is when looking at emails and returning messages can be done, rather than letting it steal time from you throughout the day.

Example 1
9:00am - 11:30am Work on priority 1
11:30am - 1:00pm Work on priority 2
2:00pm - 4:00pm Work on priority 3
4:00pm - 5:00pm Finish off any loose ends
Example 2
9:00am - 10:00am Write blog post
10:00am - 10:30am Break
10:30am - 11:00am Study
3:00pm - 4:00pm Client call
KNOW YOURSELF BETTER
What are your top 3 distractions
-At work?
-At home?
-What can you do to minimize them?
Consider your to do list right now. What 3 things are your top priorities for tomorrow? Write them down and stick to them!

If things take longer than you thought they would, it doesn't have to throw your day off track. Just make a note and adjust your expectations for next time.

Need, wants, would like
Sometimes what we have on our to do list isn't quite as pressing, but we still find ourselves with a long list and no

idea where to start, which can often result in us doing absolutely nothing. Hands up who's been there?

Need to
Want to and
Would like to.

The needs are the essentials. The food shopping, the appointment to attend, the task you've been putting off for so long that it has indeed become urgent. Although many things seem as though we need to do them, when you ask yourself "do I need to do this or do I want to do this?" you'll find that many needs and wants are confused.

See, I want to see friends for lunch, I want to buy a new dress for an upcoming wedding and I want to weed the garden but when I think about it, none of them absolutely have to be done today. The kids party, the drinks with your in-laws, they might seem like a "need to" item because you've said you'll be there but do you need to? Or do you want to? Maybe you don't at all, in which case it's an easy item to take off your list!

I find that separating out the "needs" and the "wants" is the most transformative part of this approach. Start by prioritizing and allocating time to what needs to be done and add in anything else around that. It very quickly relaxes you to know that anything essential will be taken care of and then you can spend time having fun, rather than trying to shrug off that niggly feeling that you've forgotten something important. It also helps you to be realistic about how much time you will have left over to do other things and prevents you making a wish list as long as your arm.

Lastly, consider, what are the things you would like to get done? These are even less important, and your day, your weekend or even your week won't be affected much one way or the other if you don't tick them off. You usually find yourself making an unrealistic mental list of all of the things you'd like to eat, do and see over the course of the weekend, because you are excited to have free time and spend it with those you love. However, when you recognize that they're all lovely but non essential to how much enjoyment you get from your time, it's far easier to enjoy a few and cut myself some slack.

Do what suits you
Make these tips work for you, in any way that you can. Perhaps you know that there is a particular time of day when you struggle with organization, in which case you can allocate things to your mornings, your afternoons and or evenings and leave the rest of the day more flexible. You can change how you make your to do lists and make them work harder for you. What I'm not doing is suggesting that you should schedule every minute of every day, because you'd drive yourself mad, but maybe an increase in structure might actually feel freer? It might have felt as though you had to do all of the things in the past, but practice identifying your priorities, give them the uninterrupted time they deserve and see how much more you can get done.

Chapter 35

Eliminate interruptions

You can probably relate if there is something that has held you back for years that was suddenly gone. Wouldn't it be amazing? That's how it felt for me. Imagine how many hours, weeks and months of productivity have been lost due to that problem in the course of my life. Whatever is holding you back from boosting your productivity, imagine how many promotions or business opportunities it may have caused you to miss out on. Imagine how much money you didn't earn as a result. Now it can all be gone.

That's the hope that will subconsciously give you the inspiration to make the change. And the change will happen beautifully. You confidently close email and additional distracting browser tabs. Your focus will immediately improve because there will be less distractions coming from your computer, and you begin plowing through your work at a noticeably faster pace that was your norm before. I hope this happens for you.

For you to begin reaping the benefits of improved productivity, you must start implementing the strategies in this book. The book can give you advice, but you have to work yourself to get started and implement the advice. So please don't put it off, and begin implementing and experimenting with the strategies in this book to make them work for you. And if some strategy doesn't immediately work, calibrate and adjust it to make it work for your unique situation.

For your part of this challenge, be honest with yourself and pick something you've been struggling with whether it is checking Facebook, news websites, email or YouTube, and do the same experiment as I did. For your accountability, send me an email and let me know about your results with your experiment. I'll be happy to hear from you. Just picture me cheering you on.

If you have a phone that is plugged into a wall and sits on your desk, good luck because it will be a source of unstoppable distractions and desk clutter! Just kidding, unless you truly need it for your work, either keep it unplugged or create a culture with your contacts in which you communicate through email or text, and schedule calls instead of letting people randomly call and distract you. When they call you, it is on their terms. But when you schedule a call, it is on your terms.

Don't let people randomly call you unless it is an emergency, they are clients who can pay you a lot of money, or they are your manager. Train people to schedule calls with you. I can add that it might also be a good rule to prioritize family communication. Almost everyone else can be trained to make an appointment with you, but your family can be allowed to call you at any time because family is more important than work. Just make sure they don't interrupt you too frivolously. If you plan to turn your phone off, you can give them another way to communicate with you such as Facebook (if other people don't bother you on it), Skype, or whatever you have on during the day where you don't get too many distractions or can designate for family only.

You probably dream of having the office all to yourself, but sadly you share it with others. Plus, since you got this book, I can already tell that you are awesome and that everyone in your office naturally comes over to chat with you because they want to be your friend.

One tactic people use to fend off co-workers who barge into their office or cubicle is using body language that communicates that they are not available to chat at the moment. You can do that by facing towards people with your face, but keeping your hands on your keyboard and your torso still facing your computer. This subconsciously communicates that you are focused on your current task now and can't talk.

Another thing you can do is politely say that you can't chat now, but offer a time to chat later in the day or schedule a small meeting with that person right then and there. You can also ask them when their next break is, and offer to come by their cubicle or office at that time. It's tricky because I know you want to stay "cool" and be their friend, but if you want to keep good focus and illuminate interruptions, you will need at least a little bit of discipline.

Another thing that helps some people is to work either late in the evening or very early in the morning because there are fewer people around during those times.

None of these are great solutions. The best solution is to do everything you can not to end up having to work in an environment like that.

If you own your business, the decision of office you will work in is yours, and it is something that is easy to control. If you are an employee at a company, you should tell your boss that working in a loud place is negatively affecting your productivity, and work output. See if there is anything they can do to help you. In the worst case, they might be understanding if your work productivity is lower than it would be if you worked in a quiet place.

Chapter 36

Build the Intention to Break Procrastination

Every journey to a goal begins with a commitment; a commitment to improve, to have better control of your nerves and to work with dedication and perseverance towards the end goal to eventually actualize it.

Without a strong commitment and a clear intention to achieve a certain goal, you are quite likely not going to move dedicatedly towards it. This is why your journey to breaking procrastination needs to begin with an unwavering commitment as well.

Accept Your Problem

To build a clear intention to resolve your problem, you first need to admit that you have a problem to address in the first place. Unless you acknowledge your problem, you will not fully realize its effects on your life and will not work faithfully to fix it. Accepting your problem becomes easier when you focus on how it is affecting (read: sabotaging) your life. To do that, do the following:

Analyze your daily routine starting from the time you wake up until you fall asleep and list down all the tasks you actually engage in. Do write down the time you devote to every task.

Now assess the importance of every task on the list and think about what it helped you achieve that day. For instance, if you spent 3 hours researching on your final year philosophy project in college, what outcome did you achieve after that research? Were you able to carry out a meaningful research or were you not so pleased with your findings primarily because you did not devote 3 full hours to researching on the topic? Think about whether or not every task you do daily helps you achieve anything meaningful in the end. If your end goal for the day is to earn $100, are you able to do it considering the time, you spend on your work related tasks?

Also, think about how much time you actually spend on the tasks stated on the list and how much of that time is invested in other activities. If you spent 2 hours drafting a 200 word email to a potential investor in your business, think about what you actually did in those 2 hours. Were you actually thinking about the content of the email and researched on it to ensure you draft a well-structured and effective email or did you spend 1.5 hours using social media on your phone and spent only 30 minutes doing the actual task?

Moreover, think about the tasks you plan to do daily, but somehow end up not doing. Write down those tasks and compare their importance and the outcomes they would have helped you achieved with the tasks already put on the list. If you had intended to write a blog post for your blog, email some PR firms, pitch a proposal to a potential client, do some household chores including laundry and preparing dinner and had to spend 2 hours with your family, but you ended up only writing a blog post and doing laundry, why do you think that happened? What went wrong and where did it go wrong that made you mess up your entire plan and not achieve your set targets for the day?

Once you have detailed out all the answers to the questions and have analyzed your routine, go through the account a few times and within minutes, you will realize how prone you are to procrastination and how harmful it is for you. When you compare the results you achieve every day with the desired outcomes, you will automatically realize how your habit to postpone important tasks and engage in something less meaningful but more attractive while you are working on an important task is actually a poisonous habit that is only destroying your life. This realization will help you accept your problem.

It is important to make a verbal and then a hand written declaration of this acceptance to put things out in the open. Say and write down, "I have a bad habit to procrastinate important tasks and I am going to work to break this habit steadfastly." Your declaration can be different, but the gist of it should be the same.

Make a Strong Commitment Backed by Compelling Whys

Now that you have acknowledged your problem and committed yourself to fixing it, you need to solidify your commitment and strengthen it by pegging it to a compelling why. You need to have a convincing reason or even several reasons why you need to overcome your bad habit of procrastination so you work with dedication towards your goal.

The whys associated with every goal motivate you to work towards its fulfillment because they are the reasons why you are chasing that goal. If there is no reason why you wish to break procrastination, why would you ever do that? If losing weight isn't important to you, why would you ever hit the gym and focus on healthy eating? To overcome procrastination, you need to figure out exactly why you wish to do it.

Close your eyes or even keep them open if you want and think about the biggest issue you are facing in your life right now. It could be anything that makes you feel discontent, brings you any sort of pain, or is keeping you from living a completely content and happy life. It could be your struggle with losing weight or the obstacles you are experiencing in setting up your business or how you are battling depression and the urge to give in to it or anything else that is seriously adding friction to your life and restraining you from living how you truly wish to live.

Write down your findings and if you recall your work routine and how much time you spend on actually meaningful tasks and those that only make you waste time, you will realize that procrastination is indeed a major reason why you are struggling to achieve your desired goals. Think about how your life would change for the better if you mustered up the courage to fight your temptations and beat procrastination to do actual work for real. Write down those reasons and use them to fuel your motivation to work towards your commitment to beat procrastination.

Chapter 37

Create an Action Plan to Work towards Your Goal

A goal is actually quite incomplete without a plan of action. You can never achieve your goal unless it is accompanied by a plan. Not having an action plan is often the reason why people fail to achieve their goals and end up starting from point zero every now and then. If you don't want that to happen to you again, this time devise a detailed action plan prior to working on your goal just like that.

Figure Out Why You Procrastinate

To create a foolproof action plan, you need to figure out the areas that need your utmost attention and effort. For that, you need to identify the major reasons why you procrastinate to know what keeps you from working on your goal and waste time on pointless activities.

Do you put off important tasks because you find them difficult?

Do you delay doing your work because you lack an important skill that can help you perform effectively and efficiently?

Do you procrastinate because you feel easily attracted to more attractive and relaxing tasks such as watching movies or napping?

Do you delay working on high priority tasks because you are scared of faltering and failing?

Do you procrastinate because you overestimate the time you have to work on a task and feel too confident of your ability to do it successfully on time?

Do you delay your tasks because you somehow underestimate the time it will take you to complete them?

The answers to these questions will give you clearer insight into the reasons why you procrastinate so much. Often, a combination of all these reasons leads to procrastination and often, there is a certain reason attached to the delay of a certain task.

For instance, you may delay working on your statistics assignment because you find the subject tough; but, you may end up not submitting your business proposal to a prospective client on time because you thought it would only take you an hour to draft it and you kept putting it off until the last minute only to realize in the end that you need at least 5 hours to work on it.

Think about the reason why you have been procrastinating on the respective goal that you have just set. List down those reasons and go through them a few times to better understand how they compelled you to put off your substantial tasks for a long time. You need to create your plan of action in a manner that all the tasks and steps make you manage these reasons so you don't give in to them again. Set Deadline and Incremental Goals
Next, you need to set a deadline to start working on your goal and another deadline on which its fulfillment is due.

A starting date is important so that you don't keep putting off the goal until the last minute and can battle the reason of overestimating the time to work on a task. An ending date is crucial because it helps you know when the goal is due so you don't waste another minute and get down to business right away.

Think about how much time you would need to work on your respective goal, and consider the pace at which you work. Once you have analyzed these factors, set a starting and ending date and write it down.

You now know when you must start working on it and have to complete it in due course. Your next task is to set incremental goals so you can systematically work towards its fulfillment instead of taking it as ONE, BIG Goal!
Often, people get intimidated by a goal because it is too big and feels overwhelming even one that is spread over a month. 30 days are a lot too, you know! To keep this intimidating feeling on the sidelines only, set incremental goals for yourself to slowly adjust yourself to this new transition and steadily move towards the end destination.

For instance, if your goal is to complete your 50,000-word e-book that you plan to self-publish on Amazon Kindle, but you keep procrastinating on it then your daily/ weekly incremental goals could be:
Write 1000 to 3000 words in week 1
Write 4000 to 7000 words in week 2
Write 8000 to 11000 words in week 3
Write total 15000 words in the next 3 days
Write another 5000 words in the next 3 days to make 20,000
This way you would slowly move towards your ultimate goal of writing 50,000-word e-book and get done with your goal in 3 to 4 months.

Create a Working Strategy during Your Peak Energy Time
Next, you need to create an effective strategy that helps you work on your incremental milestones and achieve them. For that, first determine your peak energy time. This is the time of the day you are brimming with energy and have the zeal to work on even the toughest of tasks.

Observe yourself and how you work on dissimilar tasks for a few days and you will start to notice a somewhat similar pattern in the way you work on different tasks at different times of the day. This will give you a clearer understanding of your peak energy time.

Your goal now needs to be to work on your incremental milestones during this time window. If, however your peak energy time is just an hour or two hour long, you need to increase it. In that case, you need to start working in small installments of 2 hours each separated by an hour long break instead of trying to do everything at once. To increase your peak energy time, take things slow and easy and don't fret on completing all your tasks in one go. With time, your willpower will improve and you will slowly inculcate the ability to work for long.

You now have to draft a strategy on how to make the most of your peak energy time so you get maximum output during that timeframe. Here is an effective plan that is quite likely to work in your favor:
Think of the goal you plan to achieve during the first week. Having that in mind, identify the different things you have to work on to fulfill that milestone.

Write down those tasks and then separate the high priority ones from the low priority tasks. The high priority tasks are all those that improve your productivity and low priority ones are tasks that don't help you achieve your goals. Create a weekly to-do list that comprises of 4 to 5 high priority tasks that you have to do throughout the week to achieve your goal. Make sure the high priority tasks are assigned for your peak energy time.

Break the weekly list into daily lists and depending on your nature, pace and the ability to handle different tasks, choose either of these two strategies. First, you do any one high priority and seemingly tough task right when the day starts. This is also known as 'eat an ugly frog' strategy and is a good technique to kick start your day and boost your productivity. However, if that is too overwhelming for you, start with a seemingly easier task and gradually move towards a toughie at the end of the day or even the end of the week so you have trained yourself to work consistently by then.

Separate all your tasks with breaks in between so you get some time to rest and rejuvenate after working on a task for even an hour. Some people, especially those who have trouble concentrating on a task for even 30 minutes straight, work for 15 minutes and then take a quick 5-minute break. You can even choose this strategy if it suits you. It is also known as the 'Pomodoro Technique' named after Italian chef Cirillo Pomodoro's tomato shaped timer. Pomodoro is Italian for tomato and as the chef used his tomato shaped timer to improve his time management skills and worked on 3 to 4 installments of 20 minutes each, the 'Pomodoro Technique' was created based on this. You too can work in this manner to make things easier for yourself.

Identify all the probable distractions that lure you away from your important chores and look for ways to manage them. For instance, if your hand unintentionally moves towards the TV remote every time you sit to work on your book, that there is your distraction that you need to overcome. If you are tempted to hit your snooze button and sleep for another hour every time you have to read articles for your thesis, that is your temptation that you have to work on.

List down your distractions and look for effective ways to manage them. If you are tempted to sleep, maybe force yourself to get up and walk for 100 steps to charge yourself so you work on the high priority task. If the TV distracts you, take it off the wall and hide it in the attic so you have nothing distracting in your room and can focus better on working. Often, our distractions are associated with the environment we sit to work in. Bringing some changes in the environment is often the trick to manage the distractions and increase our productivity.

Next, you need to start working on the first task on your list and just do it without overthinking about it. It is best to plan it beforehand right when you are creating your weekly/ daily to-do list so you know how to execute it at that time. When it is time for you to work on your to-do list, pick the first task and execute it right away. You don't have any time to think about it because that would trigger procrastination once again. Avoid that by just doing that task to save yourself from any trouble later on. If it helps, encourage yourself to work on it for 5 to 10 minutes only and keep going like that for a while. Referred to as the '5 Minute Hack', this trick mostly works well in helping you engage in a seemingly tough task and completing at least one part of it successfully.

Work on these guidelines consistently for a few days and in a couple of weeks, you will get a hang of the routine and nurture a habit of it. You now have to keep working on your weekly to-do lists to achieve your incremental milestones, one after another to move closer towards your destination.

Learn to Settle for Good Enough

Often, people who have the habit to chase perfectionism and try to do everything perfectly, find it incredibly hard to achieve their set targets. If you are a perfectionist or use perfectionism as an excuse not to work on your plan of action, you are quite likely to fall in the same trap when you try to overcome your urge to procrastinate.
Now that you have learned how to commit yourself to this goal and know how to craft an effective action plan, you need to train yourself not to allow perfectionism take over you.

To become a doer and achieve your targets, learn to settle for good enough results and not exhaust yourself trying to achieve 100% results because nothing is really perfect. Perfectionism is a myth because nothing can ever be perfect. There will always be some room left for improvement, something that could have been better; some aspect that you could have paid more attention to and some area which if you could have worked harder on would have helped you achieve better results. The truth is this is because of a glitch in your mind. You need to fix that glitch to block your negative thoughts pertinent to overthinking and perfectionism.

Here is how you can learn to settle for good enough, overcome your tendency to chase perfectionism and slowly overcome procrastination for good:
Whenever you start doing a task, think of the set target prior to tending to that chore.

Go through the steps of the tasks and set a certain time limit to work on every step. If you have to create a business logo for a client and the steps involved include researching for inspiration for an hour, working on the logo for 2 hours and making sure it complements the client's ideology and demands then make sure to work on every step for the designated timeframe only.

Start working on the steps and make sure to spend only the designated time on every step, not even a minute more. If somehow you are unable to achieve a certain step in the set time, move to the next step. If you cannot move forward without completing the prior step, take a break and tend to that chore after a few hours or the same time the next day. Once you are done with a task, analyze your performance and tell yourself how happy you are with the outcome even if you were able to achieve 50% to 60% of the set target. Smile and keep telling yourself repeatedly how pleased you are with yourself. If you do it intentionally a few times, you will eventually be happy with your performance. That said, do identify your weaknesses and work on them to achieve even better results the next time.

If you consistently work on these steps and train yourself to achieve your set targets within the set timeframe and not spend extra time on a task, you will eventually learn to settle for good enough. Your next task is to further strengthen your focus so you work with sheer dedication towards your objective.

Conclusion

Thank you for making it to the end of this book this shows me you are fully dedicated to creating a career and a life that you love.

Throughout this book, I have encouraged you to encourage yourself. At the end of the day, that's the only person you can depend upon. You need to know that your lack of productivity is a result of your approach. It isn't the fault of the person who gave you the work. It isn't the fault of someone who didn't do his share. When you are willing to take responsibility for your own lack of organization and are able to apply the above exercises to your working life, you will find you get more out of yourself and feel more motivated to keep working at that particular level of production.

Another thing that is worth remembering is that unhappy people don't work to their full potential. In other countries this is thought of as of paramount importance and employers go out of their way to make the lives of their workers pleasant. In the western world, however, it is left to the employee to find his own incentive. It's a good idea to remember that you only have one life. You need to balance it in such a way that you have all the elements of WORK, REST AND PLAY. That means making sure that you have family time. It means giving your personal life the same level of importance as your home life. There's not much point in earning millions if you never have the time to share them with your son or daughter and don't really have the energy to participate in his or her life. It's not worth being so unproductive that you lose your job either. You need to find the balance.

Although you may think that you are indispensable, the fact is that no one is. When you die, it's forever. You only get this one chance to balance your home life and your work life and if you can find that balance, you give yourself all of the incentive you need to be productive both at home and at work and can use the strategies given in this book for both your home life and your work life.

Start to see things in perspective and realize that your lack of productivity spells your lack of sensible approach. Change your approach and up the incentive and begin to enjoy your life to the fullest.

By now, you've identified your strengths, passions and values as well as some of your key personality traits and you should have a better idea of what your ideal career looks like.

You've also developed a strong mindset that enables you to make consistent progress toward your career goal until you achieve it. I guess, at this point, the only question I have left for you is:
Are you committed to designing your ideal career or are you merely interested?
Committing will make all the difference in the world. We usually know what to do but rarely do what we know. Don't read this book and forget about it. Keep moving toward your goal. If you haven't yet, go back and do the exercises and, more importantly, create your action plan.

Since motivation usually doesn't just appear, you have to figure out ways to motivate yourself and find the drive and desire to succeed. This book aims to help you to that in a quick and efficient way.

The next step is to try a few of the tips in this book to see if you can change your perspective on hard work and achieve success. It might be difficult at first to get yourself going, but once you do, you can be a force that will mean big changes for your life and those around you!

About the Author

To begin, Harib Shaqsy has been writing books for many years. He brings over thirty years of practical knowledge in his books and does coaching from time to time.

He is the author of the best seller book "Hard Work Can Keep You Poor." In his book, Harib feels that most people are over working and over stressed unnecessarily, because, they believe that working hard is the only way to survive, be paid more and become richer, he explains why this is not true in his book.

You can also check some of Harib's work available in bookshops and online.

Visit website: http://haribshaqsy.com

References

www.inc.com/john-rampton/work-smarter-not-harder-10-ways-to-be-more-effective-at-work.html

www.medium.com/the-mission/the-productive-benefits-of-doing-less-to-achieve-more-6f1998ef05a6

William Morrow, Reprint edition (January 15, 2000), Do Less, Achieve More: Discover the Hidden Powers Giving In, www.amazon.com

www.inc.com/john-rampton/work-smarter-not-harder-10-ways-to-be-more-effective-at-work.html

www.forbes.com/sites/rachelritlop/2016/12/28/6-tips-on-working-smart-not-hard-this-year/#592eeb1229f5

Ben Yagoda, "Slow Down, Sign Off, Tune Out," New York Times, October 22, 2009.

www.themuse.com/advice/kiss-your-long-todo-list-goodbye-7-ways-you-can-start-working-smarter-not-harder

L. L. Bowman et al., "Can Students Really Multitask? An Experimental Study Of Instant Messaging While Reading," Computers and Education, 54 (2010): 927–931.

https://daringtolivefully.com/do-less-and-achieve-more

www.forbes.com/sites/forbesagencycouncil/2018/01/05/want-to-work-smarter-not-harder-follow-these-14-tips/#3deef3104589

S. T. Iqbal and E. Horvitz, "Disruption and Recovery of Computing Tasks: Field Study, Analysis, and Directions," Proceedings of the Conference on Human Factors in Computing Systems, 2007.

www.lifehack.org/articles/work/dont-work-harder-work-smarter-with-these-12-tips.html

www.bakadesuyo.com/2018/02/work-smarter-not-harder-2/

www.iwillteachyoutoberich.com/blog/how-to-be-more-productive/

A. Bucciol, D. Houser and M. Piovesan. "Temptation At Work," Harvard Business School Research Paper, no. 11-090, 2011.

www.medium.com/@dsilvestre/how-to-work-smarter-not-harder-86fd6f675f01

www.wikihow.com/Work-Smart,-Not-Hard

https://hiverhq.com/blog/work-smarter-not-harder/

S. Leroy, "Why Is It So Hard To Do My Work? The Challenge Of Attention Residue When Switching Between Work Tasks," Organizational Behavior and Human Decision Processes, 109, no. 2 (2009): 168–181.

www.mindful.org/achieve-more-by-doing-less/

Walter Mischel, Ebbe B. Ebbesen, and Antonette Raskoff Zeiss, "Cognitive And Attentional Mechanisms In Delay Of Gratification," Journal of Personality and Social Psychology, vol. 21, no. 2 (1972): 204–218.

https://www.goodreads.com/book/show/952830.Do_Less_A chieve_More

R. Baumeister and J. Tierney, Willpower: Rediscovering the Greatest Human Strength. (New York: Penguin Press, 2011).

https://www.thebalancecareers.com/how-to-work-smart-9-steps-to-a-more-productive-work-day-2164686

Kimberly D. Elsbach and Andrew B. Hargadon, "Enhancing Creativity Through 'Mindless' Work: A Framework of Workday Design," Organization Science, 17 (4) 470–483.

https://www.inc.com/bryan-falchuk/want-to-achieve-more-in-your-job-these-4-simple-things-can-help.html

Murakami Haruki, What I Talk About When I Talk About Running (New York: Vintage, 2009).

https://www.thesimpledollar.com/money-mindsets-to-help-you-get-out-of-debt/

Michael Chui et al., "The Social Economy: Unlocking Value And Productivity Through Social Technologies," McKinsey Global Institute, 2012.

https://www.forbes.com/sites/ronashkenas/2012/03/12/do-less-to-achieve-more/#8da55af4ff8f

Gretchen Reynolds, "Get Up. Get Out. Don't Sit," New York Times, October 17, 2012.

https://www.everydollar.com/blog/budgeting

Linda Stone, "Just Breathe: Building the Case for E-mail Apnea," Huffington Post, February 8, 2008.

https://www.forbes.com/sites/nextavenue/2018/01/29/how-to-work-less-and-achieve-more/#7f7a570247ce

Pearce Wright, "Nitric Oxide: From Menace To Marvel Of The Decade." A briefing document prepared for the Royal Society and Association of British Science Writers, 1997.

https://www.google.com/search?q=saving+money&oq=saving&aqs=chrome.2.69i57j0l5.4981j0j7&sourceid=chrome&ie=UTF-8

Leslie Berlin, "We'll Fill This Space, but First a Nap," New York Times, September 27, 2008.

https://www.psychologytoday.com/us/blog/brave-over-perfect/201505/8-ways-achieve-more-working-less

David Lynch, Catching the Big Fish: Meditation, Consciousness, and Creativity (New York: Tarcher, 2007), 74.

https://www.entrepreneur.com/article/248050

Wikipedia contributors, "Perfectionism (psychology)," Wikipedia, The Free Encyclopedia, accessed November 16, 2012, http://en.wikipedia.org/wiki/Perfectionism_(psychology).

https://www.realmenrealstyle.com/work-less-make-more-money/

"perfectionism," Merriam-Webster.com, accessed
November 16, 2012, http://www.merriam-
webster.com/dictionary/perfectionism.

https://medium.com/swlh/how-to-be-productive-10-ways-to-
actually-work-smarter-16fea8087ead

Rao, S. (2010) Happiness at Work: Be Resilient, Motivated,
and Successful – No Matter What. New York: McGraw-Hill
Education.
https://aircall.io/blog/support/how-to-be-productive/

CPSIA information can be obtained
at www.ICGtesting.com
Printed in the USA
BVHW031412110121
597543BV00004B/71